On Earth as in HEAVEN

JUSTICE ROOTED IN SPIRITUALITY

On Earth as in HEAVEN

Arthur Paul Boers

Foreword by
Eugene H. Peterson

HERALD PRESS
Waterloo, Ontario
Scottdale, Pennsylvania

Canadian Cataloguing in Publication Data
Boers, Arthur P. (Arthur Paul), 1957-
  On earth as in heaven : justice rooted in spirituality

Includes bibliographical references and index.
ISBN 0-8361-3545-8

1. Spiritual life.   2. Spiritual life—Mennonite authors.   3. Prayer.
4. Christianity and justice.   I. Title.

BV4501.2.B63   1991   248.4'897   C90-095786-7

Scripture quotations are from the Revised Standard Version of the Bible, copyright © 1946,
1952, 1971 by the Division of Christian Education of the National Council of the Churches
of Christ in the USA. Used by permission.

Scripture quotation marked JB is from *The Jerusalem Bible*, copyright © 1966 by Darton,
Longman & Todd, Ltd. and Doubleday, a division of Bantam, Doubleday, Dell Publishing
Group, Inc. Reprinted by permission.

Portions of this book have been or will be published in the following: *Christian Living*,
January 1987, March 1987, November 1989, June 1990; "Nagging for God's Justice," *The
Christian Ministry* (all rights reserved); *Foundation Series for Youth*, September-November
1990; *The Mennonite*, September 1985; *The Mennonite Reporter*, 1989, 1990; "God's First-Strike
Strategy," *The Other Side*, January 1987 (all rights reserved); "Haiti's 'Little Church':
Thelisma Rene's Resolute Witness," *The Other Side*, July-August 1987 (all rights reserved);
"Feast of Fools: A Meditation on the Eucharist," *St. Anthony Messenger*, February 1989; "Help
My Unbelief," *St. Anthony Messenger*, August 1990.

Grateful acknowledgement is made for permission to use on p. 150, "Waiting for a Miracle"
© 1986 Golden Mountain Music Corp. Words and Music by Bruce Cockburn. Taken from
the album "Waiting for a Miracle."
On p. 154, "Feast Of Fools" © 1978 Golden Mountain Music Corp. Words and music by
Bruce Cockburn. Taken from the album "Further Adventures Of."
On p. 156, "Dweller By A Dark Stream" © 1981 Golden Mountain Music Corp. Words and
music by Bruce Cockburn. Taken from the album "Mummy Dust."

ON EARTH AS IN HEAVEN
Copyright © 1991 by Herald Press, Waterloo, Ont. N2L 6H7
    Published simultaneously in the United States by Herald Press,
    Scottdale, Pa. 15683. All rights reserved.
Library of Congress Catalog Number: 90-85237
International Standard Book Number: 0-8361-3545-8
Printed in the United States of America
Design by Paula M. Johnson/Cover art by Mary Chambers

1 2 3 4 5 6 7 8 9 10 97 96 95 94 93 92 91

To Paul and Roelie Boers
with the grateful love
of their son.

Contents

Humility
Hope and Persistence
Be Still and Know That I Am God
Timid Faithfulness

Foreword

I have not seen statistics (like the annual record-keeping we get of carnage on our highways) on the soul-wrecks of those who speak and act in Jesus' name in this pain- and sin-stormed world. But the numbers, if we had access to them, would certainly stagger us.

When we work with our fellow humans at the core and depths where God and sin and holiness are at issue, we face countless dangers, pretenses, and errors. "Spiritual" work exposes us to spiritual sins. Temptations of the flesh, though difficult to resist, are at least easy to detect. Temptations of the spirit come disguised as invitations to virtue.

Any Christian risks yielding to any of the temptations. But the hazards are especially great for those of us whose work is explicitly defined as Christian—pastors, teachers, missionaries, chaplains, activists, reformers. The very nature of the work is a constant temptation to sin. Sin is, to put an old word on it, pride. But pride disguises itself. It looks and feels like devotion, energetic commitment, sacrificial zeal.

This pride originates in a hairline split between personal faith and public ministry. In our personal faith we believe God has created, saved, and blessed us. In our public ministry we work at creating, saving, and blessing on God's behalf. We become Christians because we need a Savior. But when we minister, we act on the Savior's behalf. It is compelling work. The world suffers. Friends, neighbors, and strangers struggle. All need compassion and food, healing and witness, confrontation and consolation and redemption.

At first we root this urgent work in God. Christ's salvation motivates us. God's justice, peace, forgiveness, salvation shapes our goals. It seldom occurs to us that anything could go wrong with work so purely motivated. But something always does go wrong. In our zeal to share the Savior, we forget our need for the Savior. At first it is invisible, this split between our need of and our work for the Savior. We *feel* so well, so grateful, so *saved*. And the need is so great.

Recklessly we throw ourselves into the fray. Eventually most of us so identify our work with Christ's that Christ fades. The spotlight falls on us. Because the task is so compelling, so engaging, so *right*, we work with what feels like divine energy—until we work ourselves into the ground. The work may be wonderful, but we turn out to be less so. We become cranky, exhausted, pushy, patronizing.

Why do we get away with this? Why doesn't anyone expose our acting like gods who need no God? Arthur P. Boers blows the whistle. But he doesn't point an accusing finger. His method is gentler and more effective: he tells stories. He tells of his temptation and sin, his recovery and restoration. He tells his always-in-process story of remaining a Christian in the daily work of speaking and acting in Christ's name.

Boers attests to the huge necessities of worship and prayer in our lives. He shares his much-tested conviction that a contemplative life is not alternate to—but the root and foundation of—active life. His story refutes all who mislabel spirituality as escapism. He writes of the endless ways ministry rooted in spirituality releases energy into the world—the energy of God's grace rather than the frenzy of our pride.

—*Eugene H. Peterson*
Pastor, Christ Our King Presbyterian Church
Bel Air, Maryland

Preface

O God, thou art my God, I seek thee,
   my soul thirsts for thee;
   my flesh faints for thee,
   as in a dry and weary land where no water is.
So I have looked upon thee in the sanctuary,
   beholding thy power and glory.
Because thy steadfast love is better than life,
   my lips will praise thee.
So I will bless thee as long as I live;
   I will lift up my hands and call on thy name (Ps. 63:1-4).

For as long as I can remember, I have yearned for a deep relationship with God. Naturally, I have not always been faithful to that longing. But it remains with me, nonetheless. Closely linked to that process has been God's ongoing challenge to minister in a broken world. Both concerns weave their way through this book and I hope they also work their way through my life.

This effort reflects the intertwining of three desires. To grow in my relationship with God. To share my faith with others. To write. In this sojourn, I owe a debt of gratitude to a vast community of friends and encouragers.

Without Mark Olson and Nikki Amarantides of *The Other Side* and David E. Hostetler (formerly editor of *Christian Living*), I might never have believed that I could write. Dorothy Friesen, Harold Jantz, Margaret Loewen Reimer, and Ron Rempel also helped me along the way.

I first met Michael A. King at a Mennonite writer's conference where he was publicly trashing editors. Then he was a lowly part-time pastor and free-lance writer like myself. Now he edits for Herald Press. I do not know whom the joke is on, but I suspect all of us—and am the happier for it. He is a gentle, affirming, and truth-telling editor. My thanks.

My Associated Mennonite Biblical Seminaries thesis on "Prayer and Peacemaking" informed early drafts of this book.

There, LeRoy Friesen, Orlando Schmidt, and Marcus Smucker gave helpful support. Later at McCormick Theological Seminary, Carl Dudley, Ted Campbell, and Larry Welborn prodded me into a deeper love of the faith, the church, the Scriptures, and the pastorate.

The hospitality of the brothers at St. Gregory's Abbey calls me to deeper spiritual commitment and discipline. The Day House Catholic Worker community in Detroit continues to teach me about prayer and peacemaking.

Henri Nouwen nourished me for years, first by his writing and later with his friendship and prayers. Will D. Campbell is another mentor; his writings more than once were used by God to direct my life. Ladon Sheats steadfastly reminds me about faithfulness along the narrow way.

My pastorates, first the Lincoln United Methodist Church in Chicago, and now the Windsor Mennonite Fellowship, gave—and give—support, faith nurturing, and continual challenge to deeper discipleship. Pastoral mentors include Martha Scott, Gerald Forshey, and Menno Epp. My peers are Ted Grimsrud, David Myers, Al Moore-Beitler, John Miller, and Randy Lepp.

Kevin Abma, Jeff Fast, and Mike Vlasman are longtime, staunch, steadfast, faithful friends. Through Kevin and Jeff I now count as friends Marilyn and Janice. Others include Mark Chupp and Sharon Shumaker, Brian and Jani Dufton, Willard and Kathy Fenton-Miller, Dale Hasenick and Jo Beachy, Carol Melnick, Mark Purnell, Daryl Reimer, Mary Stewart, Ralph and Veronika Wischnewski. I love you all.

My wife of over ten years, Lorna McDougall, and our dear children Erin (six) and Paul (four) know all too well that writers do not make family life easier. Thank you all for your love, your support, your encouragement, your correction, your laughter, and your play. Special thanks to Lorna.

I am dedicating this, my first book, to my dear parents, Paul (Pleun) and Roelie (Roelofje Ganzevoort). They are forthright, hardworking, deeply loving, and long-suffering folks who uphold me always. They grow more and more important to me and I dare not imagine my life without them. Mom and Pa, I thank you and I thank God for you.

For God alone my soul waits in silence,
    for my hope is from him.
He only is my rock and my salvation,
    my fortress; I shall not be shaken.
On God rests my deliverance and my honor;
    my mighty rock, my refuge is God.
Trust in him at all times, O people;
    pour out your heart before him;
    God is a refuge for us (Ps. 62:5-8).

> *—Arthur Paul Boers*
> *Windsor, Ontario*

Introduction

I work too hard. Everyone tells me so and they're right. I know they are. But I can't help it—my work always seems so important. I know I am proud and vain. I know God can build his kingdom without me. I know I have all kinds of sinful motivations that make me workaholic. Yet I believe what I do is significant. I try to serve God's kingdom and I want to do God's will.

Where do we draw the line? Where does one stop serving God and start serving oneself? Some say we cannot love others unless we love ourselves. But how much should we love ourselves before we love others? Others tell us we cannot serve others unless we first take care of ourselves. But how much self-care do we need before we can serve others?

It always comes back to balance. We need to be both-and people, not just either-or. There are no formulas for finding our own equilibrium. Each person's answer will be different. Throughout life we struggle to find the right balance and invariably must keep readjusting the solution.

Several times in my life, my tendency to overwork has gotten me in trouble. It took obvious problems to remind me of my need to slow down. In crises, I saw that my life was off-balance and out-of-kilter.

When I was twenty-five, I had no summer job for the first time in some thirteen years. I took advantage of my free time by trying to learn all I could about the arms race, especially nuclear weapons. As well, I researched prayer for my master's thesis. I worked hard and became obsessive. Friends complained that I was spending too much time alone. They were offended that I was apparently ignoring them.

Overworked, I was not prepared for the crises soon to come. First, my studies of the arms race literally gave me nightmares. Often I would wake up dreaming of the terrors of nuclear war, visualizing the flashes of light and the mushroom clouds that

meant the end. Each time I heard a loud noise, I was afraid the
Bomb had exploded nearby. Because of my disturbed sleep, I
was not getting proper rest.

But imagined problems were not my only troubles. Early in
July, I learned a good friend of mine had been shot and killed.
Most disturbing, her husband (also a friend of mine) was
charged. Her violent death and his inexplicable involvement
greatly preoccupied me. Furthermore, my wife, Lorna, and I
were stressed that summer by our close involvement with a
couple whose marriage was falling apart.

One day, I learned more bad news. A dear friend of ours had
been raped in her bed by a prowler. What was God doing that
summer? Was God hiding? How could all these terrible things
be happening so close together? The morning I learned this
latest news, I decided to spend time praying. But even in prayer,
I could not escape the world's grim realities. I heard our four-
year-old neighbor girl screaming in terror. Trying to pray was
hopeless, so I went to the window to see what was going on. The
girl's mother yelled threats against her daughter, "I'll knock you
out!" As the girl ran through the backyard, the mother chased
her, striking her with a sandal. Not knowing what to do, I sat in
my room and cried in despair.

I felt unable to cope with everything that was happening. I did
not know how to take it all in, nor did I know what to do with
what was in my heart. Not surprisingly, I burned out. Ironically, I
had overworked myself on my prayer project to the neglect of
the rest of my life: friends, recreation, and even prayer. I violated
health, spirituality, and relationships to get something done.
Eventually, with rest, counseling, and some time off, I recovered.

More recently, the first year of my second pastorate was an
exciting one. I was no longer an assistant pastor as before. No,
now all the major pastoral responsibilities rested on my
shoulders. I liked that. I appreciated the church. I enjoyed the
community. And I liked my work. I probably liked it too much. It
was my first year and there was a lot I wanted to accomplish. So I
put in many long hours to do what I thought needed to be done.
While I cared for the church and its members, I was not taking
care of myself. People warned me, but I ignored them.

However, an amazing convergence of circumstances remind-ed me that in spite of all my Christian work I was ignoring the one I was supposedly serving. My roots were shallow. Jesus needed to send a profound reminder: "Abide in me."

I had just come through a largely affirmative evaluation of my work as a pastor. But one persistent criticism was repeated: I needed to slow down. While people commended my energy, they told me that I should not wear myself out. One evaluator wrote, "He pushes himself, possibly expecting too much too soon. I don't want him to 'burn out.' He should share some of the burden and not take on so many projects." Another noted that I should have more free time. The church's evaluation of me was the first step in my own reevaluation of my overwork. I *was* close to burning out.

I needed a break and I knew it. So I decided to visit a monastery for a few days. Years before, I had gone there once a month. For me, it is a familiar place in beautiful surroundings. Just the place for some rest and recuperation. I went gladly, look-ing forward to long quiet hours of reading, walking in the woods, and praying.

Once again, I found the monastery to be a healing place of silence and prayer. And as always, being there challenged me to be more serious about my prayer life at home. I knew I had been too busy. I had too long neglected my prayers. When I did try to pray at home, I was too tense and distracted to calm down. I felt God challenge me again to take prayer more seriously.

As I settled into my retreat, this conviction became clearer and clearer. My journal includes these simple but telling de-scriptions about what I felt while on retreat: clean, whole, rested, and at peace. Those were good feelings, but now unfamiliar as I had not experienced them in a long while.

While at the monastery, I spent a lot of time reading books by Henri Nouwen, one of my favorite authors. He writes simply, clearly, and profoundly about prayer and service. Often, his gentle, healing words put me in the mood for prayer. Nouwen's words also reminded me, *Arthur, God wants you to pray more when you return to Windsor.*

While at the monastery, I was surprised to discover that an

acquaintance now lived down the road. Gene Herr had once helped me by encouraging me in my prayer life. We had not seen each other for five years. Was it a coincidence that he was now so near me? He was part of a group that ran a retreat center. I went to visit him there. As we got reacquainted, Gene gave me a book I had never heard of, *Working the Angles* by Eugene H. Peterson. Gene insisted it was essential. Back at the monastery, I immediately began to read it and was astounded.

> Three pastoral acts are so basic, so critical, that they determine the shape of everything else. The acts are praying, reading Scripture, and giving spiritual direction. Besides being basic, these three acts are quiet. They do not call attention to themselves and so are often not attended to. In the clamorous world of pastoral work nobody yells at us to engage in these acts. It is possible to do pastoral work to the satisfaction of the people who judge our competence and pay our salaries without being either diligent or skilled in them. Since almost never does anyone notice whether we do these things or not, and only occasionally does someone ask that we do them, these three acts of ministry suffer widespread neglect.[1]

The words stared me in the face, a truthful accusation, a stinging slap on the cheek. More than that, they lodged in my heart. I knew they were an accurate analysis of where I had gone astray. I had been like a Martha. It was as if Jesus now said to me, "Arthur, Arthur, you are anxious and troubled about many things; one thing is needful. Mary has chosen the good portion, which shall not be taken away from her" (Luke 10:41-42). How did my old friend Gene know this was precisely the book I needed?

But my lessons were not over. I went home well-rested, feeling that the extended period of prayer and worship had deepened me spiritually. But all my good resolutions about a renewed prayer life were quickly washed away.

It was a cold Wednesday afternoon when I received another word from God. A word that again reminded me to slow down and change direction. I was at home, taking care of our two preschoolers. Everything was getting to me. The noise and disorganization of being with a two-year-old and a four-year-old in a normal day at home was more than I could handle. My temper was short and my harsh words to them neither gentle nor considered.

I went on the porch to fetch the mail. Paul, the two-year-old, ran out the door and onto the cement porch in his bare feet. Without thinking, I grabbed him by an arm and swung him back into the house. I did not intend to be malicious. In fact, I had swung him like that many times before.

But Paul began to cry loudly. He held his right arm as if it was hurt. And I panicked. In retrospect, I know what I should have done—gone immediately to the doctor. But I could not make up my mind to do this. Partly, I was just too ashamed. I feared that his arm was dislocated and people would consider me a child abuser. I did phone the doctor but was frustrated when I was kept on hold for ten minutes. I kept hoping that Paul's arm would get better.

After I vacillated for over an hour, his arm was back to normal. Things worked out, but my panic reminded me that I was not in control. Rather, my compulsive overwork had drained and sapped me. I was not even capable of coping with a minor crisis.

God's best and most consoling words came a few days later. Working for *The Other Side* magazine, I met and interviewed Henri Nouwen. He was living with mentally handicapped people in a L'Arche community north of Toronto. I was excited by the opportunity, since Henri Nouwen is an important influence in my life. Not knowing what to expect, I had no idea how well that occasion would be used for my own healing and recovery.

As well as conversing, we prayed together, participated in a worship service, visited with other members of the community, and shared about ourselves. He told me that there have been two voices in his life. One was ambition. The other urged him to stay close to God. I knew both voices had sounded loudly in my own life. Nouwen understood me well. We had only met, but his intuition was accurate and uncanny. He asked me why I had gone to the monastery the previous week.

"I was overtired and overwhelmed by everything. Children, work, people's problems, counseling, and busyness. This has been a pattern in my life. I go at something really hard, wear myself out, and then I have to pull back. I know my own need to find balance in my life."

Nouwen looked at me and then took a risk. "You have a tender heart. Children get to your nerves, work is so overwhelming, or counseling really gets to you, because you are very tender. But this also means that God is calling you to a deep spiritual life. That's the other side of the story. Tenderness can destroy you because you can just be pulled apart, burn out, and the whole thing. But you can also be a mystic. That's what you obviously have to be. To be a mystic, I don't mean anything more than that God is the one who loves you deeply. And that's what you have to trust. And keep trusting, keep trusting, keep trusting. . . . Otherwise everybody gets to you. Everybody's going to eat you up."

At some point in our conversation, I must have looked sad. Suddenly, Nouwen gave me a reassuring smile. He stood up, pulled me to my feet, and enveloped me in a bear hug. Throughout the day, I was grateful to have someone listen to me so sensitively and so perceptively. He affirmed me and by the time I left I felt that I had been built up.

Sometimes, perhaps, we are a little too hasty to attribute certain events to God or to assert that we know God's will. At other times, we are too hesitant to acknowledge God's intervention in and involvement with our lives. But I know that there are glimmering, shining moments of Providence when we sense God's hand. My October crisis and the evaluation, monastery retreat, *Working the Angles*, and Henri Nouwen were all ways that God called me again: Abide in me.

This book introduces prayer and its importance for those who are working for God's kingdom. This includes everyone who—by their lives, their witness, their example, their deeds, and their prayers—concretely seek to do God's will on earth as it is in heaven.

It is the vocation of all Christians to work for God's kingdom of justice and peace. "Seek first [God's] kingdom and his righteousness, and all these things shall be yours as well" (Matt. 6:33). Whether our jobs are in a church, a social agency, a home, or secular institutions, God calls us all to contribute to the king-dom.

Although the practical consequences of that call will be dif-ferent with every individual, the kingdom is a central priority for all of us. God calls us away from the destructive forces that drive and compel the world, away from competition, pride, success, prosperity, materialism. I am appalled by a TV commercial that warns, "If you're not moving up, you're falling behind."

As Christians, we are all called by God. That is the meaning of the word *vocation*. Although we are not called to do exactly the same thing, we are all called to follow Jesus and to work in his kingdom. Having this vocation means that all we do, all we are, and all we have is God's. Spirituality is about being rooted first in God's vocation. It means deriving from God our purpose, identity, direction, and self-esteem. Rather than asking the self-centered question, "What is God's will for my life?" we are em-powered to ask bigger questions, such as, "How can I fit into the work of God's kingdom here on earth?"

Instead of making rootedness in God our priority, however, we often try to justify ourselves by works. Whatever the reason, we Christians tend to be busy people. Ironically, in our frantic and frenetic attempts to be different and distinct from the world, we are often overcome by the forces of the world. While we may claim different goals, our motives for working in God's kingdom are often as selfish as our unbelieving neighbors.

But it need not be so. "In the world you have tribulation; but be of good cheer, I have overcome the world," Jesus promised (John 16:33). A major task of our growth as Christians is to learn how to trust and rely on God. Hopefully, our work on God's be-half will be rooted in God's love and grace. We will be neither compelled nor driven nor frantic. Rather, we will work with con-viction and calm, trusting God's purposes and ways.

Writing about prayer is difficult. By its very nature, prayer cannot be analyzed, itemized, or scrutinized. Prayer can only be lived and experienced. Thus these words are most helpful only if they lead the reader to a deeper experience of prayer. Prayer is deeply personal and intimate, which makes it even harder to write about.

I offer these as reflections that come from the intimacy of my own relationship with God. Thus they are based in what I experience and know. That is both their strength and their weakness. Although I believe and profess everything that I write herein, I cannot pretend that I live up to any reality or truth within these words. As much as anything, these reflections are my goals, hopes, and prayers.

It is difficult to talk about these deeply personal things. I hope that these sharings nourish you in your walk with God. Once I timidly gave a workshop on prayer and was surprised by people's response to me. They began to share all manner of personal things. At first I wondered about this, but then I realized that they felt they already knew and trusted me. We now had a relationship because I had shared deeply of myself with them during my presentation on prayer.

The greatest challenge in trying to write about prayer is the fact that it is closely related to the Holy Spirit who is far beyond our understanding and control. "The wind blows where it wills, and you hear the sound of it, but you do not know whence it comes or whither it goes; so it is with every one who is born of the Spirit" (John 3:8). Thus writing about prayer is itself a paradox. It is writing about something that cannot be taught or verbalized, but only ultimately experienced.

In gratitude for God's care for me, in the desire to encourage and nourish others, and in the hope that I—and you—will grow more deeply in prayer, I offer this book.

ONE

Abide in Me

"*Abide* in me, and I in you. As the branch cannot bear fruit by itself, unless it *abides* in the vine, neither can you, unless you *abide* in me. I am the vine, you are the branches. He who *abides* in me, and I in him, he it is that bears much fruit, for apart from me you can do nothing.

"If a man *does not abide* in me, he is cast forth as a branch and withers; and the branches are gathered, thrown into the fire and burned. If you *abide* in me, and my words *abide* in you, ask whatever you will, and it shall be done for you.

"By this my Father is glorified, that you bear much fruit, and so prove to be my disciples. As the Father has loved me, so have I loved you; *abide* in my love. If you keep my commandments, you will *abide* in my love, just as I have kept my Father's commandments and *abide* in his love. These things I have spoken to you, that my joy may be in you, and that your joy may be full" (John 15:4-11, italics added here and throughout).

Sheltered by God

My help comes from the Lord,
    who made heaven and earth.
He will not let your foot be moved,
    he who keeps you will not slumber.
Behold, he who keeps Israel
    will neither slumber nor sleep (Ps. 121:2-4).

Years ago, I learned from my grandmother's gravestone that this was her favorite psalm. It struck me as especially significant then. Eventually, I forgot about the beautiful psalm and only rediscovered it as I recently began praying through the Psalms.

As a father of small children, I appreciate the promise that "he who keeps you will not slumber." Invariably being the last one to bed, I have certain responsibilities. I need to check all the doors and ensure that they are firmly locked. I turn down the thermostat and shut off the lights. After making my appointed rounds, I quietly move upstairs.

I usually visit the children, studying their peaceful faces in the half-light. Risking waking them, I kiss them and whisper in their ears, "I love you." Sometimes they stir a little; I hope my love penetrates their dreams.

When I finally get to bed, the house is generally quiet, but I am alert. I try to ignore normal outside noises—traffic sirens, barking dogs, neighbors coming and going. I disregard the routine creaks and groans of our old house settling and shifting. Yet I listen, in case there might be an intruder in the yard or prowler in the house.

More than that, I listen to the children. Their doors are left open so that we can be attentive to their smallest whimper. Although I dearly cherish my sleep, my love and concern for the children prevails.

Children need a safe and secure home where they can take much for granted. Recently, I was discussing with Lorna the fact that I would soon be "marrying" two people. My five-year old Erin burst out in a horrified and panicked "No!" She thought I meant I was leaving our family for another. When I was her age I had never heard of divorce, but most of Erin's friends are from broken homes. The fear that her father might leave shook her to the core. She should not have to face such fears.

A little friend of Erin's was visiting. We knew her father had been laid off recently. So we asked her whether he was now working. "I guess so," she responded. Later, we learned he still was unemployed. She was secure in not knowing the pressing needs of her family. That was appropriate for one so small.

This is much like our relationship with God. The children

sleep trustingly, secure in their home and close to their parents. They have no idea what it takes to run a house or shut it down for the night. They do not need to know. They are unaware of so much. They usually do not even hear each other cry. And so it should be.

It is the nature of children to be dependent on others. So many times a day, the children ask us for help. Feed me. Clothe me. Dry me. Help me. Fix this toy. Help me to go here. Help me to do that. And while we fancy ourselves as independent, self-sufficient adults, before God we are just as dependent as children.

Psalm 121 reminds me that God attends to us, to our smallest sound and every need. While I, a relatively good parent, eventually do sleep, God never slumbers. We want to be mature, but before God we are never more than children. We wish to be his colleagues, but we remain God's creatures. I no more know my real needs before God than my children understand their real needs. If all goes as expected, they will eventually grow into maturity. But we always remain children before God.

Yet we have the privilege of prayer. God attends to us, listening for our smallest whisper or whimper. God hears us pray even before we realize that we are praying! Just as a parent ministers to a child, often before the child even realizes she is ill. "Likewise the Spirit helps us in our weakness; for we do not know how to pray as we ought, but the Spirit himself intercedes for us with sighs too deep for words." (Rom. 8:26).

Simone Weil describes her spiritual pilgrimage in *Waiting for God*. She notes that she prayed before she understood what she was doing. This surprised her. "I had never foreseen the possibility of . . . a real contact, person to person, here below, between a human being and God."[1] Yet God came and changed her life. She describes prayer as "the orientation of all the attention of which the soul is capable toward God."[2]

Prayer is the spiritual movement that helps us count on God as our shelter and help. Prayer just happened to Weil by the grace of God. She knew neither that she needed it nor that she could do it. Prayer is the God-given power that roots us in his reality and helps us to count on him always.

Dwelling with God

We have all seen them. "Aging women with swollen ankles and ulcerated feet, toting bags, shuffling slowly across the street, poking into garbage cans, slumped on a park bench, dozing in doorways, sprawling across library steps, huddled among their possessions in the dreary waiting rooms of train and bus stations."[3]

When we meet homeless people on the street, we often look away. Perhaps the stench of uncleanliness is too much. Maybe we feel guilty because of our relative affluence. Perhaps we wonder whether we should do something for that person or remain stymied by the hopelessness of the homeless. Maybe we worry that homelessness is a contagious disease and we prefer to avoid risking infection. Will a sudden crisis in our own lives force us into the same sad condition?

Homelessness is a great (and scandalous) social and spiritual crisis of our day. Tragically, it is on the rise. When my wife, Lorna, and I lived in an emergency shelter in Detroit's inner city, we were astounded by how damaged homeless people were. I later learned it is almost impossible for homeless people to be reintegrated into "normal" human society. The absence of a secure home tortures and twists their minds.

Our lives center around the search for security and often that quest is bound up with the need for a home. Yet in profound spiritual ways, we always remain homeless. And to be homeless is also to be hopeless. If we choose to reject or ignore God, then spiritually we are choosing to be homeless.

Our lost and lonely state is powerfully described early in Genesis. "The man and his wife hid themselves from the presence of the Lord God among the trees of the garden" (Gen. 3:8b). After they avoided God's presence,

> the Lord God sent [the man] forth from the garden of Eden . . . . He drove out the man; and at the east of the garden of Eden he placed the cherubim, and a flaming sword which turned every way, to guard the way to the tree of life (Gen. 3:23a-24).

Like Adam, we are lost and unable to return via that guarded route.   Ever since, humanity has been unable to make its own way back into the presence of God, into normal healthy relations with the divine. We have been wanderers, strangers, sojourners, fugitives, aliens, and pilgrims upon the earth and in the world. Like Cain, we have strayed far "from the presence of the Lord, and dwelt in the land of Nod, east of Eden" (Gen. 4:16). All people everywhere have had to make a choice about where they would dwell and live—at home in the world, or seeking to be at home in and with God.

In some senses, God has always been accessible to us and has always been our true home.

> Lord, thou hast been our dwelling place
>   in all generations.
> Before the mountains were brought forth,
>   or ever thou hadst formed the earth and the world,
>   from everlasting to everlasting thou art God (Ps. 90:1-2).

While God is everlasting, we are only dust and must learn to find our measure by God's standards.

> So teach us to number our days
>   that we may get a heart of wisdom (Ps. 90:12; cf. Ps. 39:4).

Only in God do we know true security. Only on God must and can we rely.

This World Is Not My Home

> Hear my prayer, O Lord,
>   and give ear to my cry;
>   hold not thy peace at my tears!
> For I am thy passing guest,
>   a sojourner, like all my fathers (Ps. 39:12).

The Bible is an extended account of roamings and ramblings. Everyone must choose whether to wander away from God—or away from the world. Abraham left his homeland and trekked to a new country. "By faith he sojourned in the land of promise, as in a foreign land, living in tents with Isaac and Jacob, heirs with him of the same promise" (Heb. 11:9). Ironically, God recommends that only through a certain homeless rootlessness can we find our home in God.

The people of Israel traveled through the wilderness. And even as they made their way to the Promised Land, their path often deviated and strayed away from God. Centuries later, both Israel and Judah went into fearsome exile in a strange land, because in the stability of having their own country (a homeland) they had abandoned God. It was in that very homeless exile that they had new opportunities to find their home in God.

It was not only the disobedient and unfaithful who found that the world was not their home. Jesus himself was homeless and had not even a bed to call his own. "Foxes have holes, and birds of the air have nests; but the Son of man has nowhere to lay his head" (Matt. 8:20). Jesus suggested that faithfulness to him would mean significant alienation in the world. "If you were of the world, the world would love its own; but because you are not of the world, but I chose you out of the world, therefore the world hates you" (John 15:19).

Later, the apostles wandered everywhere to spread the good news of the kingdom of God. Likewise, succeeding ancestors in the faith ranged around the world, trying to be faithful to God. Sometimes they traveled to preach the gospel and build the kingdom. At other times, they were forced to move by persecution and the need to be true to their convictions.

How could these faithful folk live without normal human security? How could they cut their roots and drift so freely? Jesus offered reassurance to those who would know suffering and even persecution in the world. "I have said this to you, that in me you may have peace. In the world you have tribulation; but be of good cheer, I have overcome the world" (John 16:33).

Spiritual homelessness in the world can be deeply tied to being at home in and with God.

These all died in faith, not having received what was promised, but having seen it and greeted it from afar, and having acknowledged that they were strangers and exiles on the earth. For people who speak thus make it clear that they are seeking a homeland. If they had been thinking of that land from which they had gone out, they would have had opportunity to return. But as it is, they desire a better country, that is, a heavenly one. Therefore God is not ashamed to be called their God, for he has prepared for them a city (Heb. 11:13-16).

The security of these pilgrims and sojourners was in God.

We are beneficiaries of the greatest of promises: dwelling with God.

> In Scripture the house, or dwelling, is presented as a means by which to make our fellowship with God assume a definite form. God also has a house; and the idea of dwelling in the house of our God is the richest thought that is given us, to set forth the most intimate and tenderest fellowship with Him . . . .[4]

While enduring temporal rootlessness, the saints of Hebrews 11 trusted that their lives were moving toward a true home with and in God.

On Earth as in Heaven

Although we are called to be migrant aliens in the world, this does not mean that we need to be lonely, abandoned, homeless, or hopeless at the deepest levels of our being. The passage from John 15, quoted at the beginning of this chapter, is a beautiful summary of our relationship with Jesus and serves as a crucial description of Christian spirituality. It is both an exciting invitation and a heartening assurance.

The best news we learn from John 15 is that Jesus chose to be intimately related to us. Even as Jesus counsels and advises us in our discipleship ("abide in me"), he gives us the great assurance that he abides in us. "Abide in me, and *I in you*." Our relationship with Jesus is not one-way but two-way, including and involving both him and us.

This mystery began with God's involvement with us on earth. Early on, God promised to be with God's people. "And I will dwell among the people of Israel, and will be their God" (Exod. 29:45).[5] A God who *dwells* among us is a God near to us. "And the Word became flesh and *dwelt* among us, full of grace and truth; we have beheld his glory, glory as of the only Son from the Father" (John 1:14).

The news about God tenting or camping with us is, in itself, astoundingly good. But the dwelling of the Word would go far beyond being merely *among* us and would come to include dwelling *in* us. Jesus was not only a neighbor on the street. Jesus promised to relate intimately to us by living *within* us.

Jesus promised that he would dwell in us through the Holy Spirit.

> "And I will pray the Father, and he will give you another Counselor, to be [KJV: *abide*] with you for ever, even the Spirit of truth, whom the world cannot receive, because it neither sees him nor knows him; you know him, for he dwells with you, and will be in you. I will not leave you desolate; I will come to you" (John 14:16-18).

With that promise fulfilled, we would be lovingly related to both Jesus and God the Father. "In that day you will know that I am in my Father, and you in me, and I in you" (John 14:20).

Many writers in the Bible shared a longing to live in and with God. The psalmists were particularly eloquent; they knew where their true home would be.

> How lovely is thy *dwelling* place,
>   O Lord of hosts!
> My soul longs, yea, faints
>   for the courts of the Lord;
>   my heart and flesh sing for joy
>   to the living God. (Ps. 84:1-2)

They pleaded with God to give them the joy of living with God.

> Let me *dwell* in thy tent for ever!
>   Oh to be *safe* under the shelter of thy wings! (Ps. 61:4)

Such were the desires of godly people. These hopes are not attainable by one's own efforts however. God's dwelling cannot be controlled by humans.

> To thee I lift up my eyes,
>   O thou who art enthroned in the heavens! (Ps. 123:1)

God is far beyond our grasp. We can neither reach nor manipulate God. "The God who made the world and everything in it, being Lord of heaven and earth, does not live in shrines made by man . . ." (Acts 17:24; cf. Acts 7:48). God "alone has immortality and dwells in unapproachable light, whom no [one] has ever seen or can see." (1 Tim. 6:16b).

How dare we even hope to approach such a magnificent being? God is far beyond us. Dwelling in and with God seems too much to aspire to. The only thing that makes it possible is God's own work.

With the events of Pentecost, God now dwells among and within the faithful. Jesus' great promise is fulfilled. "And they were all filled with the Holy Spirit and began to speak in other tongues, as the Spirit gave them utterance" (Acts 2:4). John's first epistle also offers us the assurance of God's in-dwelling.

> But the anointing which you received from him abides in you, and you have no need that any one should teach you; as his anointing teaches you about everything, and is true, and is no lie, just as it has taught you, *abide in him*." (1 John 2:27)

Paul reminds us of our motivation for holy living this way:

> For we are the temple of the living God; as God said,
> "I will live in them and move among them,
>   and I will be their God,
>   and they shall be my people" (2 Cor. 6:16).

Paul had previously cited this reminder to the Corinthians. "Do you not know that you are God's temple and that God's Spirit dwells in you?" (1 Cor. 3:16).

In Ephesians, we find this beautiful description of what God is already doing with us.

> So then you are no longer strangers and sojourners, but you are fellow citizens with the saints and members of the household of God, built upon the foundation of the apostles and prophets, Christ Jesus himself being the cornerstone, in whom the whole structure is joined together and grows into a holy temple in the Lord; in whom you also are built into it for a *dwelling* place of God in the Spirit. (2:19-22)

God is not content to dwell in and among us. He intends to do so with all peoples on earth as in heaven. In the new Jerusalem, God "will wipe away every tear from their eyes, and death shall be no more, neither shall there be mourning nor crying nor pain any more, for the former things have passed away" (Rev. 21:4). God's presence brings healing, comfort, protection, and security.

Abiding in Love

After Jesus' initiative of relatedness with us, we need to choose whether we will remain in Jesus, responding to his gracious invitation to "abide in me." Apart from Jesus' initiative in the first place, we are helpless. Only with Jesus' empowerment can we abide—"apart from me you can do nothing" (John 15:5b). This is Jesus' doing and not ours. "You did not choose me, but I chose you and appointed you that you should go and bear fruit and that your fruit should abide . . ." (John 15:16a).

But John 15 is not merely invitation and assurance. It is challenge, as well. Jesus reminds us that our deeply intimate relationship with him (abiding in him as he abides in us) is not merely comfortable. It is true, of course, that his presence can help, console, and strengthen us even in the worst of circumstances. Paul exults that nothing can "separate us from the love of God in Christ Jesus our Lord" (Rom. 8:39).

But the Bible's assurance of God's loving presence serves as a warning that we will need those very helps. The implications of the good news of God's dwelling among us go far beyond warm fuzzies. We have done nothing to earn Christ's abiding presence among us, and we cannot make ourselves worthy to abide in Jesus, but there are, nevertheless, expectations of us.

It is possible to reject the great gift of residing in Jesus. We can choose to be vagrants of the spirit. We can cast off God's garments of praise and God's shelter of love, choosing instead the cold streets of self-preoccupation. Thus we are warned in 1 John 2:28, "And now, little children, abide in him, so that when he appears we may have confidence and not shrink from him in shame at his coming."

Likewise Paul admonished and encouraged his churches to nurture God's abiding presence. "Let the word of Christ dwell in you richly . . ." (Col. 3:16a). Paul also says, "Guard the truth that has been entrusted to you by the Holy Spirit who dwells within us" (2 Tim. 1:14).

If we abide mutually with Jesus, there will be results. "He who *abides* in me, and I in him, he it is that bears much fruit, for apart from me you can do nothing" (John 15:5b). In fact, the bearing of fruit, the following of God's commands, are the signs of our relationship with and in God. "By this my Father is glorified, that you bear much fruit, and so prove to be my disciples" (John 15:8).

Jesus has expectations of us and abiding in him means obedience to him. "If you keep my commandments, you will abide in my love, just as I have kept my Father's commandments and abide in his love" (John 15:10). Obedience to Jesus reflects his prior obedience to God. "He who says he abides in [Jesus] ought to walk in the same way in which he walked" (1 John 2:6).

Jesus' rule or command is well-known: it is love, nothing more or less. "This is my commandment, that you love one another as I have loved you" (John 15:12; 14:15-21; cf. Mark 12:28-34). Love shows whether or not we abide in God. Love is the sign and fruit of the integrity of our discipleship. "He who loves his brother *abides* in the light, and in it there is no cause for stumbling" (1 John 2:10).

A healthy relationship with God means that we will walk in love. It is not enough to have the correct doctrinal beliefs. God is not first a God of theology, philosophy, or theory but a God of active and redemptive love. We are called to no less. Our love comes from God and is enabled by God and God alone.

The Paradoxes of Abiding

Our faith in God and God's faithfulness to us launches us into many paradoxes. Even as we find ourselves homeless in the world, we are invited to security with and in God.

Even as our dwelling with God is not our doing but his, we too are called to take responsibility for our life with him. Even as God's abiding presence gives security and blessing, that same redemptive love calls us to expose ourselves to the dangers and risks of loving others as well.

> Blessed is the man who trusts in the Lord,
> whose trust is the Lord.

He is like a tree planted by water,
    that sends out its roots by the stream,
    and does not fear when heat comes,
    for its leaves remain green,
    and is not anxious in the year of drought,
    for it does not cease to bear fruit (Jer. 17:7-8).

Rooting ourselves in God does not mean that we escape the heat and drought of adversity and suffering. In fact, our acts of faithfulness may attract hostile responses from the world. In that sense, choosing to dwell in God means asking for trouble. But God invites us into the truly tremendous joy of abiding in and with our Maker and Sustainer.

Prayer is a crucial way we take refuge in God. In prayer, our spirits are brought into the safe and secure home for which they were created. In prayer, we know and trust that God acts on our behalf in ways that are beyond our ken. In prayer, we are like little children who can rest in God.

In prayer, we may even begin to discern the muffled shufflings of our Parent through the darkened house late at night. Perhaps we feel more than hear our divine Lover moving about. And ever so gently we feel the brush of lips on our cheeks and the wonderful words whispered in our ear: "Rest easy my child, for I am with you and I love you, I abide in you and dwell with you." And we dare sleep soundly, "since he provides for his beloved as they sleep" (Ps. 127:2b, JB).

TWO

Who Is God?

In our discussion of God abiding in us and our opportunity to abide in God, we have not yet considered a crucial question. As we think about prayer, it is vital that we know God's identity. Who is this God that we follow? What does God tell us about God's self? To know God, we look first at God's self-revelation.

Some time ago, I took a course on prayer, hoping to grow in this vital and essential area of my life. But I was troubled by what I heard in the class. My well-meaning teachers kept speaking vaguely about God, saying things such as "whoever God is for you." This tends to focus on what we think, on what we would like, on our projections of God. Spirituality must be rooted primarily in God's revelation to us. When God is revealed to us, in mystery and paradox, in confusing symbols, in inexplicable metaphors, we encounter a God who leaves us uneasy and challenged.

The Bible is one of the most important resources for our lives as Christians. Yet it is becoming less and less influential. In Canada, more people read the horoscope than the Bible. One friend of mine, Tom Yoder Neufeld, is a New Testament professor. Once he was staying at a bed-and-breakfast place and was asked by his host what he did for a living. "I teach religious studies."

"What's that?" his host asked. "I studied Eastern religions."

"No, this is biblical studies," Tom replied.

"Biblical?"

"You know: the Bible."

"The Bible—oh, you mean that Gideon book!"

That host is similar to many today. He may be an expert on other religions, he may understand God as "whoever God is for you," but he does not know the Bible.

Through the Bible, God specifically addresses us and teaches us about who God is. We sometimes have exalted ideas about where we can find God. Each of us has preferred methods. Some look for God in beautiful buildings. Others search for God in nature. Some listen for God in rousing music. Others quest for God in beautiful liturgies.

Any of these may be pointers to God. But they could just as likely be idols. We need to look first where God tells us to look. Too often our spiritual pointers point us up to a projected God and away from the world. But God clearly tells us to look around on earth.

Scriptures show that God has special priorities of love for the poor and justice for the oppressed. Any spirituality that aims to help us abide in God must take seriously God's identification with the destitute. Thus our prayer lives will affect our lifestyles and change the way we relate to those whom society scorns and rejects. Faith that draws us into relationship with the God of the Bible also draws us into involvement with the world, endeavoring to flesh out God's kingdom and will on earth as in heaven.

God the Social Justice Legislator

The Spirit of the Lord is upon me,
because he has anointed me to preach good news to the poor.
He has sent me to proclaim release to the captives
and recovering of sight to the blind,
to set at liberty those who are oppressed,
to proclaim the acceptable year of the Lord (Luke 4:18-19).

In the Bible, issues of wealth and poverty, hunger and justice, oppression and freedom are central. Again and again, comfort is offered to the poor, warnings to the rich, and judgment to oppressors. God specifically aided the weak and needy by giving the Israelites a series of laws that reflected his priorities of social justice. Some of these seem strange and unusual in our culture today, yet they are still relevant. To this day, God desires to establish his priorities on earth as they are in heaven.

In the Old Testament, God instituted many laws concerned primarily with the care and welfare of the poor. For example, the law of gleaning forbade farmers to reap to the edge of their fields. They were also not to collect or pick crops after the harvest.

Why not? The leftovers (or gleanings) at the field edge and after the harvest were for the most needy in Israelite society—foreigners, orphans, and widows. Thus Ruth (both a foreigner and a widow) was given the privilege of gleaning in the field of Naomi's relative, Boaz (Ruth 2:2ff.).

With this rule, God made sure that every crop would be used to feed the poor, the hungry, and the helpless (Lev. 19:9-10; Deut. 24:19-22).

Today, this is still being creatively practiced. When I worked in an inner city shelter and soup kitchen in Detroit, we relied on a food bank named "Gleaners." From stores and restaurants, it collected food that was not marketable for various reasons (e.g., it was mislabeled or the packaging was slightly damaged). For a nominal price, the food bank sold the food to organizations that served the needy. These leftovers fed the poor, rather than being left to rot in a dump.

Another law, tithing, also helped strangers, orphans, and widows. One tenth of all farm crops were to be set aside, given for the care of priests (Levites) and the poor. The destitute had a legal right to expect to be fed (Exod. 22:5; Deut. 23:19-20; Lev. 25:35-8). God guaranteed this right in laws God framed for the people.

The discipline of setting aside a portion of one's income was both spiritual and social. It reminded people of the deeper truth, "The earth is the Lord's" (Ps. 24:1). Tithing does not show that God owns one-tenth of our possessions. Rather, it reminds us that God owns everything and we are only stewards of God's possessions. The tithe represents God's total and complete ownership.

Similarly, Israelites were not allowed to charge interest on loans. Meeting the needs of the afflicted was more important than making profits (Exod. 22:25; Deut. 23:19-20; Lev. 25:35-38). These days that sounds strange, as we are accustomed to an economic system that relies on charging interest. Yet it is interest that often crushes the needy.

During the Middle Ages, the church forbade the taking of interest, which was called *usury*. Jews were allowed to be moneylenders so Christians could remain "pure." Shylock in Shakespeare's *The Merchant of Venice* is probably the most famous medieval moneylender.

Habitat for Humanity is a much-celebrated organization which builds low-cost homes for those in need. It began humbly building homes in a rural setting in Georgia. Then it spread to the third world and finally came back to North American cities. Thousands of needy people now own homes because of the work and efforts of Habitat for Humanity.

Following Old Testament laws against usury, a major rule of Habitat for Humanity is the refusal to charge interest. The main reason poor people cannot afford mortgages is because of the interest, which over the years usually adds up to more than the principal itself. Purchasers of Habitat homes receive interest-free loans. Over a twenty-five year period, regular and affordable payments are applied entirely against the principal, enabling needy people to purchase homes.

Canadians and Americans are increasingly worried about deficit spending. But we are not yet too sensitive about third world debts. Developing countries are over one trillion dollars in debt. In 1989, a group of African church leaders met with some North American counterparts in New York. "Banks need their money and governments need their power; in the meantime our children are dying. If we pay this debt we would be worse off than colonization," said Tshimungu Mayela, a pastor from Zaire.[1]

Our siblings in the third world are understandably concerned about this. Trying to pay their international debts often means reversing progress and development. Children are among the most victimized. The result is that countless thousands of young children die each year, school enrollment declines, health expenditures are cut, and malnutrition rises.

Thus Old Testament laws against charging interest remain relevant today. The world does not need more people to subscribe to "whoever God is for you." The world is crying and hungry for the same Lord God who thousands of years ago enacted and enforced laws on behalf of the poor and impoverished.

Every seven years, God wanted Israelites to observe a Sabbath year. During this time, farmers were not allowed to plant, tend, or harvest crops. Rather, everything that grew that year was to be given to the poor (Exod. 23:10-11). This benefited many people and was also good for the soil.

Furthermore, during this Sabbath, all debts were to be canceled. The law demanded that loans also be routinely made to the poor during the sixth year, even though the chance of repayment would be slim (Deut. 15:1-11). Finally, Hebrew slaves were to be freed during the Sabbath year.

We are more familiar, of course, with the notion of a Sabbath day. This was itself a protective social measure, intended for the good of laborers. This humanitarian law guaranteed social equality and regular rest from endless work. It even included animals (Deut. 5:13ff.). Today, our obsession with consumerism has made every day of the week a shopping day. Not many places now enforce the old "blue laws" against Sunday shopping. But labor unions reflect God's priorities when they insist that laborers and their families need a common day of rest.

Another special law was the Jubilee, scheduled every fifty years. We do not know whether it was ever observed. When God gave Canaan to the Israelites, each family received a portion of the land. God knew some families would eventually lose their lands and others would acquire those lands. Thus every fifty years the land was to be redistributed evenly according to the inheritance of one's ancestors. This was to keep a privileged few from permanently getting wealthier at the expense of others.

The famous story of Naboth's vineyard turns on this law and explains why Naboth refused to turn over his land to King Ahab. "The Lord forbid that I should give you the inheritance of my fathers" (1 Kings 21:3).

These laws were of primary concern to the prophets. When they raged against the injustices of their day, they often remembered the Exodus. They reminded the Hebrews that they too had once been a slave people, foreigners without land, oppressed by others. The prophets remembered that these and other laws were intended to protect and aid the weak in their society.

Thus, for example, Jeremiah pleaded for the observance of the Jubilee year (Jer. 34). Whenever the prophets denounced oppression and called for justice, they acted in the spirit of these laws, assuming that all are entitled to food and the basic physical and material necessities. The prophets knew that one of God's highest priorities is social justice.

Jesus reflected God's concern for the needy. For example, he wanted the Sabbath observed *justly*. "The sabbath was made for man, not man for the sabbath; so the Son of man is lord even of the sabbath" (Mark 2:27-28).

The Jubilee was a prevalent theme in Jesus' teaching and life. The quote that opened this section, "to proclaim the acceptable year of the Lord" is a reference to the Jubilee. Jesus saw that his mission was to initiate the Jubilee. Mary also reminds us of the Jubilee in her prayerful Magnificat (Luke 1:52-53). Even the Lord's Prayer—the model of Christian prayer—echoes Jubilee themes. "Forgive us our debts, as we forgive our debtors."

Thus God through Old Testament laws, prophets' passions, and Jesus' teachings and example clearly reveals the divine concern to legislate on behalf of the poor and needy. When we pray to God, we pray to someone who expects us to honor and respect the needs and rights of the downtrodden and the oppressed. As affluent North Americans, we are tempted to create a God that makes us feel comfortable in our lifestyles. Instead, the Bible reminds us that God expects our lives to do justice on earth, as it is done in heaven. Perhaps the foreignness of those Old Testament laws reveals how far our society has moved from the Lord God of the Scriptures.

God the Advocate for the Poor and Oppressed

And God said to Moses, "I am the Lord. . . . I have heard the groaning of the people of Israel whom the Egyptians hold in bondage and I have remembered my covenant. Say therefore to the people of Israel, 'I am the Lord, and I will bring you out from under the burdens of the Egyptians, and I will deliver you from their bondage, and I will redeem you with an outstretched arm and with great acts of judgment, and I will take you for my people, and I will be your God; and you shall know that I am the Lord your God, who has brought you out from under the burdens of the Egyptians' " (Exod. 6:2,5-7).

God tells us still more about God's identity. God is not just some liberal legislator levying laws from on high. (Nor does God expect us to work through justice only through the political manipulation of legislation.) God does not only tell us how to live and act on behalf of the oppressed in the giving of laws. On earth and in history, God acts out his passionate concerns.

God is intimately involved in the process of salvation and justice. God is revealed as an advocate—even a warrior—on behalf of the poor.

You shall not afflict any widow or orphan. If you do afflict them, and they cry out to me, I will surely hear their cry; and my wrath will burn, and I will kill you with the sword, and your wives shall become widows and your children fatherless (Exod. 22:22-24).

During Israel's captivity in Egyptian slavery, God was intimately concerned about the injustice and suffering that the people endured.

And the people of Israel groaned under their bondage, and cried out for help, and their cry under bondage came up to God. And God heard their groaning, and God remembered his covenant with Abraham, with Isaac, and with Jacob (Exod. 2:23-24).

In those first words to Moses from the burning bush, God showed feelings about the Israelites' enslavement and promised to free them. "I have seen the affliction of my people who are in Egypt . . . and I have come down to deliver them out of the hand of the Egyptians" (Exod. 3:7-8). God was not aloof from their suffering but moved by it.

God acted decisively to free these poor slaves. The book of

Exodus is an eloquent testimony of how God is an advocate and warrior for the oppressed. Exodus 15:1-18, possibly the oldest segment of Scripture, praises the Lord God who is a warrior: saving enslaved Israel from Pharaoh and the other exploiters.

> The Lord is a man of war;
>   the Lord is his name (15:3).
> Who is like thee, O Lord, among the gods?
> Who is like thee, majestic in holiness,
>   terrible in glorious deeds, doing wonders?
> Thou didst stretch out thy right hand,
>   the earth swallowed them.
> Thou hast led in thy steadfast love the people whom thou hast
>   redeemed,
> thou hast guided them by thy strength to thy holy abode (15:11-13).

Thus from Israel's earliest history, God is identified as one who freed an enslaved and oppressed people.

Every year, at the harvest feast of first fruits, Israelites rehearsed and celebrated God's action. "And the Egyptians treated us harshly. . . . Then we cried to the Lord . . . and the Lord brought us out of Egypt with a mighty hand and an out-stretched arm, with great terror, with signs and wonders" (Deut. 26:6-8).

God is the ally of the dispossessed and the oppressed. "For I the Lord love justice. . . ." (Isa. 61:8). "For thou has been a stronghold to the poor, a stronghold to the needy in his distress. . . ." (Isa. 25:4; cf. Ps. 9:9). Over and over, the Bible shows us God's priorities.

> O Lord, thou wilt hear the desire of the meek;
>   thou wilt strengthen their heart, thou wilt incline thy ear
>   to do justice to the fatherless and the oppressed,
> so that man who is of the earth may strike terror no more (Ps. 10:17-18).

God does not sit aloof in heaven, apathetic to the trials and tribulations of those on earth (Ps. 107). No, God hears and feels the violence and injustice that is perpetrated. Thus in response to the first murder, God says, "The voice of your brother's blood is crying to me from the ground" (Gen. 4:10).

God is not deaf to the outraged and beseeching moans of those who are victims on earth. "The cries of the harvesters have reached the ears of the Lord of hosts" (James 5:4). When people are oppressed, violated, and abused, perhaps they feel alone, that no one cares. But there is one who always hears, always cares, and perpetually longs for shalom everywhere.

But God does not only hear the suffering. God acts on behalf of those who are in need. "I know that the Lord maintains the cause of the afflicted, and executes justice for the needy" (Ps. 140:12). This is how God is known. "And this is the name by which he will be called: 'The Lord is our righteousness [justice]' " (Jer. 23:6). God protects the poor, for "the Lord is his refuge" (Ps. 14:6).

When Israel did not honor God's priorities, the Lord's concern for justice took on startling dimensions. In time, God judged Israel through heathen agents of retribution, Assyria and Babylon. When Israel forgot her own beginnings and oppressed others, Yahweh's anger and judgment turned against her. Thus the prophets warned that injustice and oppression would lead to punishment and even exile (Amos 6:4,7; Hos. 9:1-3; Isa. 10:1-4; Mic. 3:12; and Jer. 5:26-29).

These truths are evident in the New Testament as well. Mary's Magnificat resounds with Old Testament themes of liberation as she sings God's praise.

> He has shown strength with his arm,
> he has scattered the proud in the imagination of their hearts,
> he has put down the mighty from their thrones,
> and exalted those of low degree;
> he has filled the hungry with good things,
> and the rich he has sent empty away (Luke 1:51-53).

Her prayer does not sound like ones I am accustomed to hearing in church.

Jesus' teachings were good news to the poor (Luke 4:18; cf. Matt. 11:5; Luke 6:20). His ministry showed an active involvement with the afflicted and despised—prostitutes, tax collectors, demoniacs, and lepers. Jesus also demonstrated his concern for the poor by warning the wealthy (Luke 6:24-25; 8:14; 12:13-21;

16:19-23). Jesus' brother James wrote one of the Bible's most stinging denunciations of the rich (James 5:1-6). Clearly, Jesus was and remains an advocate for the forgotten.

Later, Paul also promoted the cause of the needy. His letters gave instructions about stewardship (1 Cor. 16:1; 2 Cor. 8—9; Gal. 2:10). A major focus of his work among the Gentiles was raising relief for the poor in Jerusalem. He risked returning to Jerusalem so that he could deliver the collection. Tradition has it that his commitment and resolve ultimately ended with his execution.

God the Poor One: The Prince Is a Pauper!

> Then the righteous will answer him, "Lord, when did we see thee hungry and feed thee, or thirsty and give thee drink? And when did we see thee a stranger and welcome thee, or naked and clothe thee? And when did we see thee sick or in prison and visit thee?" And the King will answer them, "Truly, I say to you, as you did it to one of the least of these my brethren, you did it to me" (Matt. 25:37-40).

We struggle to know God and grow spiritually. In our search, we have so far learned surprising things about God's connections with oppressed people here on earth. God was concerned enough to enact legislation for their protection. God went further, actually fighting on behalf of the downtrodden. But the mystery of God is deeper. God is found among the poor. God identifies with the poor. The way we treat the poor person on earth is intricately connected with the way we treat God.

This should not be entirely surprising. In Genesis, we learn that God created humans in the divine image. Each human being potentially reflects God. Each violation of a fellow human, someone made in God's image, offends God. We cannot know God directly, but we can relate to God in our treatment of each other. "No [one] has ever seen God; if we love one another, God abides in us and his love is perfected in us" (1 John 4:12; cf. 4:7-8).

We know and love God by responding to our neighbor with love. There is no other way to love God. "If any one says, 'I love God,' and hates his brother, he is a liar; for he who does not love his brother whom he has seen, cannot love God whom he has not seen" (1 John 4:20). There is no distinction between the social and spiritual here. The way that we treat our visible neighbor parallels our spiritual relationship with the unseen God.

Jesus, of course, already established this when he connected the two great commandments with each other.

> You shall love the Lord your God with all your heart, and with all your soul, and with all your mind. This is the great and first commandment. And a second is like it, You shall love your neighbor as yourself. On these two commandments depend all the law and the prophets (Matt. 22:37-40).

Likewise, Paul summarized all commandments in the formula, love your neighbor as yourself (Rom. 13:9; Gal. 5:14). Thus we love God by loving our neighbor. God is found and known in our neighbor. God is honored in the way we treat others.

Because of God's care for all humans, because God has created all people, because God desires us to love one another, God personally feels it when any humans are devalued, harmed, or violated. Thus it is no surprise that God cares especially for people who are oppressed or abused.

Throughout the Old Testament, knowing God is closely related to acting justly. "So you, by the help of your God, return, hold fast to love and justice, and wait continually for your God" (Hos. 12:6). Waiting for God is spiritual terminology we often use in Advent, but here Hosea shows that the waiting for God is not only passive, it actively loves and does justice. Jeremiah rebukes a king with the example of his father.

> Did not your father eat and drink
> > and do justice and righteousness?
> Then it was well with him.
> He judged the cause of the poor and needy;
> > then it was well.
> Is not this to know me? says the Lord (Jer. 22:15-16).

The king's father showed that he knew God in the fact that he did justice for the poor and needy.

God identifies himself with those who need justice. Injustice violates humans (the image of God) and thus violates God (Gen. 10:6). "He who oppresses a poor man insults his Maker, but he who is kind to the needy honors him" (Prov. 14:31).

Why did I never learn this when I was growing up? How has the church missed this important idea? "He who mocks the poor insults his Maker. . . ." (Prov. 17:5). Our dealings with the poor connect directly with our relationship to God.

We have the promise of a future when all will know God. That knowledge will mean a world of shalom, a new creation of peace and justice.

> They shall not hurt or destroy
> in all my holy mountain;
> for the earth shall be full of the knowledge of the Lord
> as the waters cover the sea (Isa. 11:9; Hab. 2:14).

Is this the knowledge of God that we proclaim and reveal in our evangelism? God is known in peace, in righteousness, in compassion. When people truly know God there is no hurting or destroying, no violence or oppression.

This is even clearer as we look at the meaning of Jesus Christ's incarnation. God, in Jesus, gave up the comfort and privilege of being God. He came among us as one of the lowly and meek. "For you know the grace of our Lord Jesus Christ, that though he was rich, yet for your sake he became poor, so that by his poverty you might become rich" (2 Cor. 8:9).

Paul eloquently writes about this when he notes that Christ Jesus, "who though he was in the form of God, did not count equality with God a thing to be grasped, but emptied himself, taking the form of a servant, being born in the likeness of men" (Phil. 2:6-7).

Jesus' life on earth was not particularly notable, at least not in materialistic terms. He was born in an unimportant country. The legitimacy of his birth was in question. His first visitors included shepherds, particularly disreputable people in that society. His family was forced to flee as refugees to Egypt. Later, as an itinerant teacher, he had no visible assets. "Foxes have holes, and birds of the air have nests; but the Son of man has nowhere to lay his head" (Matt. 8:20).

Jesus identified with the bereft and the impoverished: "Truly, I say to you, as you did it to one of the least of these my brethren, you did it to me" (Matt. 25:40). Later, when Saul had his vision, he learned first-hand of Jesus' identification with the oppressed. "And [Saul] fell to the ground and heard a voice saying to him, 'Saul, Saul, why do you persecute me?' " (Acts 9:4).

Mother Teresa is one of the most famous Christians in the world today. People are awed by her devoted service to the dying of Calcutta. It is widely reported that she understands her practical work as an expression of her spirituality. She sees Jesus in those she ministers to.

Where do we go to see Jesus? To church or a soup kitchen? To a monastery or skid row? To a Bible camp or a housing project? I suspect that the answer is not either-or, but both-and. But woe, woe to anyone who would try to see God in heaven without loving the needy on earth.

Many devotional materials I read focus on the greatness and inscrutability of God. We describe God as all-knowing (omniscient), all-powerful (omnipotent), and everywhere (omnipresent).

While those attributes of God may inspire reverence, they can also be a distraction. For God calls us to look elsewhere for him. If we are interested in biblical spirituality, then we should ponder God as poor, hungry, accused, imprisoned, in debt, unemployed, leprous, oppressed, disinherited, handicapped, devalued, needy, destitute, mourning, persecuted, prosecuted, outcast, scorned, despised, gook, commie, bum, disheveled, disreputable, retarded.

THREE

Implications of God's Identity

Poverty Incarnate

It is unsettling to directly confront poverty, just as it is unsettling to meet God. One summer morning at 6:30 a.m., I was driving home after bringing a friend to the airport. I was about twenty miles from home when I spied a hitchhiker. I hid the money that was on my dashboard as I pulled the car over. A thin man with a shaved head climbed in.

I searched for things to talk about. So I told him about my morning—a long and funny story about an absent-minded housemate almost missing his plane. As I mentioned certain words—fly, limousine, airport—I wondered whether this could amuse someone who had probably never had a chance to fly. He did not laugh. He did not respond at all.

I realized how little we had in common. Bill took a conversational initiative by complimenting my car. "Thanks," I said. But I felt ill at ease. My car, a telling sign of my relative wealth, also reinforced the gap between us. Each time one of us would say something, it was followed by a long silence. When we finally got around to names, I learned he was Bill and "glad to know" me. I was "pleased to meet" him. He kept forgetting my name and calling me "Ken."

I was surprised to learn that he lived in the Gospel Mission. He was even more transient than I first guessed. Through my work, I met many Mission residents and they all hated it. But Bill was different. "It's a good place." I wondered whether he might be religiously inclined.

Out of the blue, Bill started talking. "If you hadn't picked me up, I guess they would have had to drag me home."

Why was that?

"Cause my foot is hurting bad. It's got a lot of bad places."

I assumed no doctor was helping him; Bill probably could not afford one.

We drove past a large, impressive-looking church and I drew it to his attention as something to talk about.

But Bill had a more pressing issue to pursue. "Are you a Christian?"

I hesitated before telling him that I was. This was the first time in my life I found myself unwilling to profess my faith. All the other times, I could brag of my faith and demand that others be converted to be like me. This occasion, however, offered a new possibility—my own conversion. Unable to make small talk, I was also unwilling to share deeply. But now the secret would be out. I would be anonymous no longer. Bill would have a claim on me.

I turned the question back. "Why do you ask?" *Do I look like a Christian?*, I wondered. Has God marked me so that everyone will know how I should behave? Before he replied, I asked another question. "Are you a Christian?"

"Yes, I'm trying to be. It's real hard. If only I could get myself straight." Several blocks of silence later, he added, "But I'm okay."

I asked how he became a Christian. "I didn't like where I was and I wanted to change for the better. What made you decide to be a Christian?"

Now I was stumped. It had been years since anyone asked for my testimony. I faltered. "I guess . . . I was brought up in a family that believed and I always believed too. Then in university, I had a lot of problems and decided that I didn't believe. But then . . . but then I remembered the stories about Jesus and knew that I believed them. So I believed."

Bill affirmed me. "That's good. That's real good."

Later, he added, "It's hard to believe sometimes. It's hard to believe even though you know. Sometimes you don't know . . . but you always know. It's real hard."

Bill asked me where I went to church. When I told him, he exclaimed in happy surprise, "You and me were almost buddies! You know Jim Penner in First Mennonite Church? He talked to me about your church and I thought about it."

I talked about the good worship, the friendly people, and how the congregation challenges me to be a better Christian.

He thought about that. "Is that right? That's good." Then a long pause. "Challenge you, huh? That's good. I never thought about it, but I guess I knew a church should do that, challenge you."

Then Bill added in a small and guilty voice, "I smoke."

"That's okay."

"I'm a Christian and still smoke, but someday the Lord will take it from me," Bill said.

I wondered if Bill was hungry. He mentioned eating the night before but sounded vague. He had already missed breakfast at the Mission. Besides, he had broken some of their rules and might not be admitted at all. So I offered him a meal. Bill accepted, adding, "I need a bath. I step out sometimes. I went out a few days ago."

By now, we were near my house. I considered eating there. We had plenty of food. Then Bill could wash up and I could give him some clean clothes. Did I want him in the house, though? What would my housemates think? Truth be told, I did not want Bill to know where I lived. He might return another day with requests or demands. So we drove right by my house and I said nothing—betraying Bill, my home, myself, and my faith.

We went to a nearby diner. It was crowded, but Bill found us a small table in a corner by the window. An overhead pipe dripped on our table and the sun shone in my eyes. The waitress came and took our orders. Bill began to thank me profusely. I tried to quiet him, feeling embarrassed. Later, he thanked me again, saying he wanted to repay me.

I was short with him. "You're welcome, please don't mention it." I was uneasy, knowing how little I was really doing.

Bill lifted the steaming cup of coffee to his lips, spilling some on his shirt and on the table. I dried the table with a napkin. He gripped the cup in both trembling hands and tried again, still dripping coffee on himself. When he finished it, he told me in disgust that he did not want more.

The food arrived and I bowed my head, quickly and silently. Bill sat there, unsure of himself. I asked whether he had family.

"I do . . . but I'm going to say I don't."

So I inquired about people at the Mission. He told me of one staff person he particularly liked and eagerly invited me to come to one of their daily Bible studies.

At one point, I asked whether breakfast tasted okay. "Yeah," but two spoonfuls later, he told me, "I'm full."

His plate was not yet half empty, but I did not lecture about waste and world hunger.

Bill turned in his chair, looking forlorn and even scared. He seldom looked at me, never in my eyes. He was even more reticent and ill at ease than he had been in the car. I asked if he was okay. He said he was. I studied his face, trying to figure out his age and trying to understand him. His face seemed young, but I could not tell whether he was twenty or thirty.

I tried joking. "I brought you here because I thought you were hungry, but it turns out that I'm hungrier than you!" No response.

Bill pointed out a man across the restaurant—someone he worked with two months ago in a steak house where Bill washed dishes. The guy was a cook and a nice co-worker. The cook walked over and spoke to someone at the next table. Bill waved but the man did not respond.

"Mr. Robinson," he called, but there was no answer. As Mr. Robinson walked away, Bill waved at the retreating back. "See," he said to me.

Bill started lamenting about not being able to straighten out. "I wish I was wise."

I had little to offer. "I wish I knew what to tell you, but I don't know what to say."

Finally we returned to the car and I again asked if he was okay.

"Yes. Cigarette smoke gets to me sometimes. There was too much smoke in there." Nevertheless, a few minutes later, he speculated, "I'm going to see whether I can get a cigarette from one of the guys at the Mission."

Once more, Bill told me, "I really want to repay you some-day."

"Look, when you have the money to repay me, you help someone else. Jesus said that whatever we do to a brother is done for him. You have Jesus in you and I have Jesus in me. Whatever I do for you, I do for Jesus and whatever I don't do for you . . ." I hesitated ". . . I don't do for Jesus."

I stopped. Jesus was present in this man and I had refused him. Here I had refused to take Jesus home or give him a bath or share my clothes.

Bill seemed not to notice my hypocrisy . . . or perhaps he did. "You talk like the Bible study teacher at the Mission. He told me that a couple of days ago, because I had a fight. There's a Scrip-ture . . . there's a Scripture passage . . ." but he interrupted him-self and pointed out the window. "Just let me off at the corner."

We were near the Mission. I drove to the front door. A num-ber of Mission residents were standing outside the door, staring at us. Bill was home. He shook my hand, got out of the car, and walked into the door.

I went to my home, left to ponder the unsettling learnings about myself and my relationship to God.

Fleshing Out God's Identity

Happy is he whose help is the God of Jacob,
whose hope is in the Lord his God . . .
who keeps faith for ever;
who executes justice for the oppressed;
who gives food to the hungry.
The Lord sets the prisoners free;
the Lord opens the eyes of the blind.
The Lord lifts up those who are bowed down;
the Lord loves the righteous.
The Lord watches over the sojourners,
he upholds the widow and the fatherless; but the way of the wicked
he brings to ruin.
The Lord will reign for ever, thy God, O Zion, to all generations.
Praise the Lord! (Ps. 146:5-10).

The Bible has long been a source of renewal, strength, and comfort for oppressed people. Larry Towell is a Canadian photographer and poet who often journeys to Central America. There, he interviews many people. One Guatemalan Indian catechist told Larry of the hardships they endured. He described how

> we had fled the army massacres, and were hiding for six years in the mountains, jungle ravines, and caves. We couldn't camp near water because that's where the civil patrol came looking. We had no guns to hunt with, so we tried to catch animals with our bare hands. Whatever we planted in crops, the civil patrol would find and destroy. It was very hard with no shelter in the mountains. Half of us died—the women and children especially, from hunger, snake bites, and, of course, from the guns of the civil patrol. I'm a catechist. The only thing I brought with me was my Bible, and the only thing I brought out was the Bible.[1]

From what we have seen above, it is no surprise that the Bible was this poor man's most treasured possession.

Our brief Bible study has shown us who God is, as God reveals through the testimony of Scriptures. Not God as "whoever God is for you." We cannot know God directly, but know and love God through our neighbor, especially our needy neighbor (1 John 4:12).

The Bible (on behalf of God) is preoccupied with issues of economics and justice. In the early 1970s, a seminary student decided to cut out of the Bible every Bible passage that referred to justice for the poor. Gone were many of the prophetic writings, snipped was most of the Psalms, deleted were many of Jesus' parables and most famous sermons. "When he was all through, that Bible was literally in shreds. It wouldn't hold together; it was falling apart in our hands."

Jim Wallis used to use the Bible as a preaching prop. "I'd hold it high above American congregations and say, 'My friends, this is the American Bible—full of holes from all that we have cut out.' " He sadly concludes that the "poor have been cut out of the Word of God."[2]

Sadly, we Christians have become masters at ignoring and distorting the Bible. Two famous humorists—who did not

profess our faith—were even more challenged by the Bible than
we are. W. C. Fields claimed that he spent years studying the
Bible, looking for a loophole. And Mark Twain once said, "It's
not what I don't understand about the Bible that bothers me; it's
what I do understand."

We are God's representatives on earth and are expected to
have our ears attuned to the cries and afflictions of suffering
neighbors. Biblical spirituality, then, is far more than saying
private, personal prayers, or enjoying the stirring worship of an
ecstatic congregation.

God taught us to look for God in history. Since knowing God
means to do the things that make for peace, even today we can
look around expecting to see God at work. When John the Baptist had questions about Jesus' identity, he sent his followers to
ask, "Are you he who is to come, or shall we look for another?"
(Matt. 11:3).

Jesus did not answer with elaborate theology or an in-
tellectual defense. He invited John's disciples to report what
they witnessed. "Go and tell John what you hear and see: the
blind receive their sight and the lame walk, lepers are cleansed
and the deaf hear, and the dead are raised up, and the poor have
good news preached to them" (11:4-5).

Jesus is loosely quoting Isaiah 35:4-6. It is these acts of mercy
and justice that show who Jesus really is. Our God is involved in
history as Psalm 146 proclaims at the beginning of this section.
When we want to know where God is active, we look for God's
compassion, justice, healing, and *shalom* at work in the world.

There is a strong thread in the Bible that expects to see God
act in history, on behalf of the needy, the oppressed, and the violated. When the kingdom is advanced, people give praise to
God. When Elijah is used to bring to life the son of a gentile
widow, she knows that God is revealed. "Now I know that you
are a man of God, and that the word of the Lord in your mouth is
truth," said she (1 Kings 17:24). Similarly, when Jesus raises the
dead son of a widow in Nain, "They were all filled with awe and
praised God. 'A great prophet has appeared among us,' they
said, 'God has come to help his people' "(Luke 7:16, NIV).

But our spirituality is not only a matter of trying to see where

God works. We cannot be content to be observers only. Biblical spirituality is not an armchair event. God's activity calls for our response and conversion to a life of faithfulness. I have heard of a pilgrim that searched everywhere for God. His travels brought him to many different people who practiced all manner of religions. In one monastery, he asked a monk, "Does your God work miracles?"

The monk did not ponder long: "It depends on what you mean. Some people like to think a miracle is when God does our will." The monk was first referring to those who subscribe to the God-whoever-he-is-for-you attitude.

But he had a healthier alternative. "Here we believe that it is a miracle when people do the will of God."

God communicates in a way that is always a question to us. "You know this about me. Now what will you do? Will you obey or will you rebel? Will you follow me or will you go your own way? Will you love your neighbor or will you oppress and do violence? Or will you just ignore the needy?"

Most religions demand that we show faithfulness through rituals. But the God of the Bible is more concerned with living justly. To believe in God is far more than proper doctrine or devout piety. Rather, to believe in God and God's kingdom means to live in a different reality than the world. Where the world sees nothing wrong in competition and materialism, we are called to lives of service and discipleship, compassion and mutual aid.

It is not enough to profess our faith with words. Our lives reflect the content of our convictions and prayers. Thus those who profess faith in the incarnate God live in ways that incarnate God's peace and justice, on earth as it is in heaven. As we turn more and more toward God in prayer, God will turn us more and more to the needs of our neighbors.

Whose Side Are You On?

We have seen that God has a special interest in the plight of the bereft and the poor, the weak and the vulnerable. This conclusion may not seem startling to some. In fact, for many it aligns neatly with the conclusions of liberation theology. And while liberation theology says much that needs to be said and while my research has been bolstered by some fine liberation theologians, I remain uneasy about some of liberation theology's major emphases.

An area of special concern is the whole matter of God taking sides. In high school, I was once discussing a certain war with a teacher. I told her that the outcome was due to God being on the side of the victors. She was surprised. "Do you really think God takes sides in a war?"

"Why, of course," I answered. It was not until years later (when I became a Mennonite and embraced the peace position) that I felt uneasy and embarrassed about my assertion.

Does God really take sides? The answer is both Yes and No. God does take sides. But God does not take sides the way we do. Many of my activist friends frequently put me on the spot when they ask me, "Whose side are you on?" That little question is intended to be a litmus test of political correctness.

Because of God's priorities, I am passionately concerned about issues of poverty and suffering, justice and oppression. I know that God longs for shalom. I know that institutions and systems victimize and trample innocent people. For that reason, I strive to be on God's side and cooperate with God's special interest in the poor.

But that does not mean poor persons are automatically my authority. The Word of God as revealed through Scripture and the life of Christ are my highest authorities. If poor people demand that my loyalty to their side means doing something against God's will (for example, practicing violence or hating their enemies), then I must disagree. They may then accuse me of being on the other side.

Being on the side of the poor does not mean that I idealize or romanticize poor persons. I have worked and lived too long in poor communities to believe that the poor are somehow better than the rest of the world. They may have a few extra credits in God's eyes, but they are as sinful, selfish, and deluded as the rest of the world.

Our primary job is not to join sides in the partisan worldly divisions that separate the world. "For he is our peace, who has made us both one, and has broken down the dividing wall of hostility" (Eph. 2:14). When we try to live that out, we tend to be suspected and accused by all sides. During World War Two, a fledgling effort to have a Mennonite church in Windsor failed partly because of the hostility to German speakers. Mennonites were not on anyone's side during World War Two. Yet because of their pacifism and language they were suspected of being Nazi sympathizers.

It is possible to be on people's side without doing what they want us to do. It is possible to serve people without doing their bidding (as any pastor, prophet, or preacher knows).

My concern here is that loose talk about being on God's side quickly becomes pious-sounding crusade talk about just revolutions or class struggles. Those committed to third world issues suggest that we get off the backs of the poor. That is a concern I readily share. We should not be accomplices in oppression. Likewise, it is not our job to dictate to the poor. But it is also not our task to join the poor in any or all tactics.

Our task is to be God's agents in a world that is all too eager to write off certain groups. Lutheran Bishop Medardo Gomez of El Salvador has sometimes been accused of advocating liberation theology because of his brave advocacy on behalf of the oppressed. But he also raises some questions about that movement.

> In fact, he is not fully sympathetic to liberation theology, objecting, for example, to the stock liberationist phrase about "God's preferential for the poor" because it excludes the rich; he prefers to speak of giving "special attention to God's children most in need."[3]

I live a great distance from most of my relatives, since both of my parents are immigrants. I have been able to visit the land of my ancestors, the Netherlands, on many occasions, however. And because of those visits I feel a sense of kinship with my relatives there. While I can feel affections for my relatives, I remain distant from their disputes and conflicts. I can be friends with relatives who dislike each other.

Ironically, my family's neutrality on this side of the ocean means that sometimes two opposing parties can separately approach us for help. They can trust us. Had my parents remained in the Netherlands, we would probably be drawn into such conflicts and only exacerbate them. We can have concern for all our relatives, and a desire for love and justice, without necessarily taking sides.

In matters of justice, we can be for the poor without identifying completely with everything that the poor do, demand, or say. In matters of the world's conflicts, we can expect to be misunderstood and accused of being on the other side. To the Zealots, Jesus was a passive accomodationist. To the Romans and other authorities, he was a subversive threat. Jesus deliberately made decisions that alienated him from those who most wanted his allegiance.

> "So Jesus also suffered outside the gate in order to sanctify the people through his own blood. Therefore let us go forth to him outside the camp and bear the abuse he endured. For here we have no lasting city, but we seek the city which is to come" (Heb. 13:12-14).

FOUR

Prayers
Are Not Enough

The Prophets Attack Spirituality

> Take away from me the noise of your songs;
>> to the melody of your harps I will not listen.
> But let justice roll down like waters,
>> and righteousness like an ever-flowing stream (Amos 5:23-24).

It may come as a shocking surprise to us, but God often opposes spiritual disciplines. We have seen that God is known in doing justice and by delivering justice to suffering neighbors. This has important implications for all our spiritual rituals, disciplines, and devotions.

Old Testament prophets spent a lot of time attacking the religious practices of their day. In fact, they spent more time denouncing devotional habits than they did explaining how to pray! An important part of their vocation was to resist what many did in God's name. This seems a strange function for God's representatives.

Reading the prophets, one might easily conclude that they were irreligious or antireligious because they attacked everything that the Israelites literally held sacred. For example, they indicted sacrifices (Isa. 1:10-16; Jer. 6:18-21; Hos. 8:13). Hosea specifically contrasted knowledge of God with burnt offerings.

Therefore I have hewn them by the prophets,
I have slain them by the words of my mouth,
    and my judgment goes forth as the light.
For I desire steadfast love and not sacrifice,
    the knowledge of God, rather than burnt offerings (Hos. 6:5-6).

According to the prophets, God goes even farther by rejecting certain prayers as worse than useless!

When you spread forth your hands,
I will hide my eyes from you;
even though you make many prayers,
I will not listen;
your hands are full of blood (Isa. 1:15).

The implication is that we cannot directly approach God by
prayer on any terms we please. Our approach is always condi-
tioned by God himself.

Prophets did not only attack human religious efforts and initiatives, but even went against God's gifts. The Temple was first
given as a covenant sign by God, but it too is ultimately condemned: "Therefore I will do to the house which is called by my
name, and in which you trust, and to the place which I gave to
you and to your fathers, as I did to Shiloh" (Jer. 7:14).

Shiloh was utterly destroyed and the Temple's fate would be
the same. It is ominous enough that God rejected religious practices initiated by the people, for example sacrifices.[1] But for God
to reject God's own work, God's own covenant sign, is beyond
comprehension.

Why did the prophets reject religious rituals on God's behalf?
Not because they were necessarily done the wrong way. If that
were so, the prophets could have criticized the incorrect practices and recommended the correct way of doing things.

Neither are the prophets criticizing wrongful attitudes behind
the disciplines. Again, if that were the case they would only have
to advocate appropriate attitudes. Nor do their criticisms mean
that some rituals are worthless while others are essentially good.
The list of condemned practices include every imaginable discipline—sacrifices, Sabbaths, prayers, feasts, solemn festivals,
chanting, and music (e.g., Isa. 1:11-16; Amos 5:21-23). Nothing

is spared. We might conclude that the prophetic criticisms show that God opposes all religious ceremonies and rituals. But that misses the point of what God is trying to communicate.

What is criticized by the prophets is a magical attitude toward rituals.[2] The Hebrews believed that certain ceremonies and institutions guaranteed them security and preservation, access to Yahweh, and defense against enemies. Jeremiah warned against such delusions regarding the Temple. "Do not trust in these deceptive words: 'This is the temple of the Lord'" (Jer. 7:4). The Temple in itself—even though it was a gift of God—promised no security.

In spite of what we struggle with in today's society, the biblical concern was not faith in God versus atheism. Rather, it was a contest between true and proper spirituality versus pagan faiths, ones that only pretended to honor God (such as idolatry). The prophets seemed antireligious because they denounced the idolatry that others considered faithful or religious. Since we know God by doing justice, we cannot manipulate God through religious rituals. Idols are subject to our machinations and maneuverings, but not the Most High God.

The issue then is not whether one sincerely seeks God or whether one attempts to perform the right deeds or the correct rituals. The question is whether or not we look for God in ways God instructed us. Idolaters and practitioners of magic believe they can approach God in any context. But that is not what biblical faith professes. The Old Testament shows that the context of our lives is relevant to our relationship with God.

As well as advocating social justice legislation, God forbade the inhuman and unjust rituals of other faiths, including sacred prostitution (Deut. 23:18), human sacrifice (Lev. 20:2-4), and spiritualism (Lev. 20:6). This was also why many of Israel's feasts celebrated justice, including the sabbatical year, the Jubilee, the Sabbath day, the feasts of weeks and tabernacles (Deut. 16:9-14).[3]

Injustice and worship could not coexist in Israel's faith. Religion that coexists peacefully with injustice is false faith, deception, and idolatry (Jer. 5:31; 7:9-10; 8:11; Mic. 3:5; Ezek. 13:10). God's priority of justice determines the righteousness, or "rightness," of rituals.

This does not mean that rituals and disciplines are unimportant. Rather, it warns of what is most important: justice before ritual. Thus, after condemning worthless religious rites (sacrifices, burnt offerings, incense, Sabbath, solemn assembly, feasts), Yahweh tells us what is nearest to the divine heart.

> Wash yourselves; make yourselves clean;
> remove the evil of your doings
> from before my eyes;
> cease to do evil,
> learn to do good;
> seek justice,
> correct oppression;
> defend the fatherless,
> plead for the widow (Isa. 1:16-17).

Biblical spirituality is rooted in a life and ministry of practicing good, striving for justice, overcoming oppression, protecting the vulnerable, and advocating on behalf of those who are powerless.

Jesus Versus Spiritual Disciplines

Jesus continues the Old Testament tradition of criticizing contemporary religious rituals and institutions. He too was sensitive about idolatry and passionately concerned that God not be worshiped as an idol. He was against manipulating God by the right words, the correct formulas, or the proper rituals. Prayer must never be regarded as a foolproof mechanism that forces God into a preordained response.

> "And in praying do not heap up empty phrases as the Gentiles do; for they think that they will be heard for their many words. Do not be like them, for your Father knows what you need before you ask him" (Matt. 6:7-8).

Time and again, Jesus made clear that obedience and justice are more important than devotional propriety. Otherwise, prayer becomes magical and misleads us into thinking that we can gain access to God on our own terms, rather than on God's terms.

Magic is going to church so you will get to Heaven. Magic is using Listerine so everybody will love you. Magic is the technique of controlling unseen powers and will always work if you do it by the book. Magic is manipulation and says, My will be done.[4]

The problem is that magic suggests that God must be subservient to our prayers. If we do it the right way, then God must obey us. Frederick Buechner goes on to point out that true prayer is not magic; rather, it is summarized in the Lord's Prayer, "Thy will be done."

I once attended a workshop entitled "Using Intercessory Prayer to Build Your Church." The very title of this presentation seemed suspicious to me. It smacked of making prayer into manipulative and magic technique geared toward effectiveness and results.

We do not use prayer for our ends, but through prayer we submit ourselves to God and the living possibility that God will use us. Prayer means that we live on and by God's terms, not God by ours. We are not being manipulated or exploited by God. We freely accept this participation on God's terms.

But prayer has the great potential to change us, often in ways that we might not prefer or even desire, turning us upside down and inside out. Its consequences are anything but predictable, let alone comfortable. Prayer does not primarily change external circumstances for our selfish benefit. It instead becomes God's opportunity to change and convert us for the sake of the kingdom.

I shared these concerns with other members of the workshop, suggesting that the presenter's point-of-view flirted with manipulating God. One brother piped up, "I am not worried about manipulating God since God cannot be manipulated."

He was right, of course. However, he missed the point. To think or act like we can manipulate God is what the Bible considers idolatry.

When I was in my first year of university, a high school friend called me to his home for a special meeting. Dan had a burden for a mutual friend, John. He hoped John would be converted to Christ. We discussed his hope, and Dan announced a plan to me. "I know how we can make John convert."

"Really? How?" I wondered.

"The Bible teaches that 'if two of you agree on earth about anything they ask it will be done for them by my Father in heaven.' Matthew 18:19. If you and I agree to pray together for John's conversion, then it will happen. Guaranteed!"

While Dan's hopes were well-intentioned, he was wrong. First, Jesus' promise refers to church discipline. More important, prayer is not something which predetermines that God must do our will. We do not know the outcome of prayer. If we pray, then the only guaranteed result is that we will have prayed. Only God can give the fruits and only God knows what those fruits will be.

Soren Kierkegaard writes:

> The immediate person thinks and imagines that when he prays, the important thing, the thing he must concentrate upon, is that God should hear what he is praying for. And yet in the true, eternal sense it is just the reverse: the true relation in prayer is not when God hears what is prayed for, but when the person praying continues to pray until he is the one who hears, who hears what God wills. The immediate person, therefore, uses many words and, therefore, makes demands in his prayer; the true man of prayer only attends.[5]

Kierkegaard's insight is too important to be ignored. Prayer is essentially intended to put ourselves in right relationship to God.

> Prayer is surrender—surrender to the will of God and cooperation with that will. If I throw out a boathook from the boat and catch hold of the shore and pull, do I pull the shore to me, or do I pull myself to the shore? Prayer is not pulling God to my will, but the aligning of my will to the will of God.[6]

Jesus had important reasons for his concern. He knew that it was easy for humans to get their priorities confused—observing trivial rules but overlooking God's requirements.

> "Woe to you, scribes and Pharisees, hypocrites! for you tithe mint and dill and cumin, and have neglected the weightier matters of the law, justice and mercy and faith; these you ought to have done, without neglecting the others. You blind guides, straining out a gnat and swallowing a camel!" (Matt. 23:23-24).

Obedience is more important than ritual rectitude, political correctness, or even theological propriety. "Not every one who says to me, 'Lord, Lord,' shall enter the kingdom of heaven, but he who does the will of my Father who is in heaven" (Matt. 7:21).

Jesus' priorities of justice and mercy are revealed in both his teachings and his example. "Go and learn what this means, 'I desire mercy, and not sacrifice.' For I came not to call the righteous, but sinners" (Matt. 9:13; cf. Matt. 12:7). In this same spirit, Jesus raided the Temple which was used to exploit others (Matt. 21:13).

Jesus valued human welfare over religious observance. Thus he deliberately broke strict Sabbath laws to feed hungry disciples (Matt. 12:1-8) and to heal (Matt. 12:9-14). "The sabbath was made for man, not man for the sabbath; so the Son of man is lord even of the sabbath" (Mark 2:27-28). Mercy for one's sibling is more important than fulfilling legalistic requirements (Matt. 12:7; 9:13; Hos. 6:6).

For Jesus, concern for others is key to our spirituality. If we are not at peace with our brother or sister, it is wrong even to worship. "So if you are offering your gift at the altar, and there remember that your brother has something against you . . . first be reconciled to your brother, and then . . . offer your gift" (Matt. 5:23-24). We cannot worship God when we are alienated from a sibling.

Jesus further criticized the prayers of hypocrites, who love to be seen acting religious. He warned against deliberately courting affirmation through public prayer. Such have already "received their reward" (Matt 6:5). This egocentric kind of prayer only glorifies self. It does nothing to build the proper kind of relationship between oneself and God or between oneself and one's neighbor.

Jesus taught that prayer, worship, and spirituality are intended to make us concerned for others, not self-centered. In Luke 18:9-14, the self-righteous prayer of the Pharisee is contrasted unfavorably with the prayer of the sinful tax collector. Jesus specifically focused this parable against "some who trusted in themselves that they were righteous and despised others" (Luke 18:9).

Clarence Jordan wryly notes that "they both got their prayers answered. The old publican asked for forgiveness and that's what he got. The old Pharisee asked for nothing and that's what he got." [7]   The Pharisee's prayer was really directed to himself. He was worshiping himself. God was omitted from that prayer.

Jesus' criticisms of religious devotions show that his highest priority for spirituality was that it teach us humility, mercy, justice, and concern for others. Without those vital elements, spiritual disciplines are worse than useless.

FIVE

The Politics
of Spirituality

The Political Nature of Biblical Faith

Seek the Lord while he may be found,
call upon him while he is near;
let the wicked forsake his way,
and the unrighteous man his thoughts;
let him return to the Lord, that he may have mercy on him,
and to our God, for he will abundantly pardon.
For my thoughts are not your thoughts,
neither are your ways my ways, says the Lord.
For as the heavens are higher than the earth,
so are my ways higher than your ways
and my thoughts than your thoughts. (Isa. 55:6-9).

Biblical spirituality directly challenges us. We are called to follow God, but this means to act in ways that do not come natural
to us. God's ways and thoughts are not our own. As we saw in
the last chapter, the prophets summoned us to remember that
our lifestyles are more accurate indicators of spirituality than our
devotional habits.

The disparity between our professions of faith and our lives
of little faith is apparent to prophets and non-Christians alike.
The glaring hypocrisy of so many self-professed Christians is a
major reason Christianity has such a bad name today.

But not only the scandals of televangelists betray us. When
the Christian handling of materialism, affluence, self-centered-

ness, and racism is no different than the world's, it is hardly surprising that others do not believe our bold claims about the resurrection and the kingdom. If we truly follow God, our lives and communities must certainly change. We ought to be different than the world if we embrace the resurrection reality of Jesus' good news.

Biblical spirituality is clearly political in its impact, implication, and implementation. By *political* we do not suggest that spirituality is Marxist or capitalist or aligned with some other ideology. Rather, we mean that spirituality is public, not just private and personal. Its implications go beyond the confines of our hearts.

Jesus criticized piety that was self-centered rather than other-directed. True spirituality, rooted in the biblical story, is political. William Stringfellow writes that

> so many of the biblical symbols are explicitly political—dominion, emancipation, authority, judgment, kingdom, reconciliation . . . and . . . the most familiar biblical events are notoriously political—including the drama of Israel the holy nation, the Kingdom parables in Christ's teaching, the condemnation of Christ as King of the Jews by the imperial authorities, the persecutions of the Apostolic congregations, the controversies between Christians and zealots, the propagation of the book of Revelation.[1]

We must not confuse the political nature of spirituality with the fallen politics of other nations. We are not calling for "a power politics based on coercion . . . [but] a politics of God, whose law for the new community was founded upon the gospel, God's act of selfless love for mankind."[2] Politics is central to the biblical understanding of spirituality. "If this political character is lost, the essential significance and relevance of Christian worship and faith are lost."[3] Biblical spirituality does not settle for individualized expressions of piety that pretend to be apolitical.

Our God Reigns!

How beautiful upon the mountains
are the feet of him who brings good tidings,
who publishes peace, who brings good tidings of good,

who publishes salvation,
who says to Zion, "Your God reigns" (Isa. 52:7).

Many regard worship as the climax of personal spirituality and piety. Although much of our worship is in the community context of a congregation, we often evaluate Sunday morning experiences only by what they do for us individually. We return home after church and ask ourselves, "Was I inspired? Was I lifted up? Was I encouraged? Did I feel God's presence?" Our individual feelings become the standard by which we judge our worship. But that falls tragically short of the biblical view of worship.

A better evaluation of worship would show concern for the political reality of God's will. Was God's gospel proclaimed? God's kingdom furthered? God's will made clear? God's grace celebrated? Did we share concerns about the downtrodden, suffering, or oppressed? Were we drawn into deeper commitment and loyalty to God's will and ways?

Questions about our own inspirations and feelings have some validity. But they overlook the main point of worship. Millard C. Lind offers a surprising insight here. He notes that "Christian worship should be defined as the celebration of the rule of God as experienced in the life of the new community in Christ."[4] In other words, worship is an explicitly political act.

But, we protest, we believe in the separation of church and state! The pulpit ought not be connected with politics. Thus we Mennonites, for example, often exclude national flags from our sanctuaries. From the beginning, the Mennonites' Anabaptists forebears advocated a radical freedom from the coercive ways of Caesar.

Those concerns are appropriate and valid. But they do not mean that Christianity is otherworldly and separate from the mundane concerns of earth. Rather, we are concerned that patriotism or national security not dictate, define, or confine our faith.

We distinguish ourselves from worldly political loyalties because our allegiances differ. We are citizens of the kingdom of God. Each worship service should draw us into deeper and deeper fealty to God and away from the petty loyalties and partisan divisions of the world. It is little wonder then that governments throughout history and around the world have often spied on and persecuted churches.

Worship is central to our lives as Christians. Indeed, it is the reason the Bible was written. "The Bible is composed largely of material which originally was formed for and used by the community of faith in its corporate worship."[5] The most important facet of Israel's life as a nation was its worship. "It is significant that the fundamental institution of this nation was an institution of worship."[6]

Worship was the primary political reality of Israel and was in fact the element that united diverse tribes. "Practically all biblical scholars today accept the view that pre-kingship Israel, while organized as separate tribes, was unified by a common worship center."[7]

At first, Israel was not even a country as we understand that concept today. It did not have a centralized government but was a loose coalition of tribes. They joined together whenever they had a project to do or a challenge to meet. They did not have a human king. But they were bound together by a common faith continually renewed in their worship life together.

From the earliest times, the people of Israel believed God was their king. Exodus 15 is an ancient poem, perhaps the oldest text in the Bible. In it, we see this important declaration: "The Lord will reign for ever and ever" (Exod. 15:18). The emphasis on God's kingship is repeated often in the Bible.[8] For this reason, the country of Israel had no human king for many years. With God as king, they needed no human king. In fact, to choose a human sovereign would have been to betray God.

At first when leaders were needed, God chose judges to accomplish specific tasks. But Israel was not always happy with this arrangement. They suspected a human king would be more helpful and effective. When certain problems arose, they tried to make Gideon, the capable judge, into a king. He refused. "I will not rule over you, and my son will not rule over you; the Lord will rule over you" (Judg. 8:23). Gideon knew that Israel's true king was the Lord.

All of Israel's worship reinforced the understanding of God

as king. Thus the covenant, the laws, the tabernacle, and sacrifices were all political.[9] Israel gathered to worship God as their Commander-in-Chief and to hear God's commands, God's laws, God's sovereign directives. The ark was seen as God's throne.[10]

The betrayal of this tradition came most tragically when Pilate brought Jesus before his enemies, saying, "Behold your King!" (John 19:14). Their rejection of Jesus showed that God's place had been completely usurped. "We have no king but Caesar" (John 19:15).

New Testament worship was a continuation of the understanding that God is king. This is reflected in the language believers used about Jesus.

> They confessed that Jesus is Lord. They proclaimed that He was at the right hand of God, the place of authority in the universe. His authority also was with them since He was with them in the Spirit.[11]

Jesus is called "Christ," a political designation which means "anointed one, coming ruler."[12]

> Therefore God has highly exalted him and bestowed on him the name which is above every name, that at the name of Jesus every knee should bow, in heaven and on earth and under the earth, and every tongue confess that Jesus Christ is Lord, to the glory of God the Father (Phil. 2:9-11; cf. Acts 2:36; Isa. 45:23; Rom. 14:11).

Indeed, this worshipful confession of Jesus' political sovereignty is also our authorization for evangelism.

> And Jesus came and said to them, "All authority in heaven and on earth has been given to me. Go therefore and make disciples of all nations, baptizing them in the name of the Father and of the Son and of the Holy Spirit, teaching them to observe all that I have commanded you; and lo, I am with you always, to the close of the age" (Matt. 28:18-20).

Note that Jesus' political authority is not only in heaven, but also here on earth.

> Thy kingdom come,
> Thy will be done,
> On earth as it is in heaven (Matt. 6:10).[13]

Herod was correct in his suspicion that the Bethlehem boy-child was a threat to his throne (Matt. 2). Jesus would establish a superior throne.

We sometimes lose sight of the fact that Jesus was subversive to the political powers of his day.

> Most churchfolk in American Christendom, especially those of a white, bourgeois background, have for generations, in both Sunday School and sanctuary, been furnished with an impression of Jesus as a person who went briefly about teaching love and doing good deeds: gentle Jesus, pure Jesus, meek Jesus, pastoral Jesus, honest Jesus, fragrant Jesus, passive Jesus, peaceful Jesus, healing Jesus, celibate Jesus, clean Jesus, virtuous Jesus, innocuous Jesus.[14]

This truncated vision of Jesus, while containing some truthful elements, fails to note that Jesus was a threatening and disruptive presence in his day.

It was no accident that Jesus was accused of political crimes and executed by the political powers-that-be (Luke 23:2). All four Gospels report that Pilate asked Jesus one particular political question, "Are you the King of the Jews?" (Mark 15:2; Matt. 27:11; Luke 23:3; John 18:33). His response was not satisfactory then, and there is no reason to believe that Jesus would be comfortable with political realities now. But the death of Jesus did not end the struggle between his kingdom and the world's kingdoms.

In fact, the gospel of Jesus is at war with the politics of this world. "As in the Old Testament, so also in the New: the chief antagonists of the biblical faith are the governments of this world."[15] It has always been so and will always continue to be so. "This conflict of the kingdom of God against the kingdoms of this world is found throughout the Bible. . . . When the church neglects this conflict, she loses her relevancy."[16] Jesus modeled a politics radically different from—and opposed to—the world's way.

> And Jesus called them to him and said to them, "You know that those who are supposed to rule over the Gentiles lord it over them, and their great men exercise authority over them. But it shall not be so among you; but whoever would be great among you must be

your servant, and whoever would be first among you must be slave of all. For the Son of man also came not to be served but to serve, and to give his life as a ransom for many (Mark 10:42-45).

Jesus' advice, though not overwhelmingly embraced by the world, has nevertheless shaped and changed the world. "You see, the times are past when the powerful and prominent alone were men, and the others—human slaves and serfs. We are indebted to Christianity for this."[17]

The confessional creeds that we find in the New Testament use explicit political language. "Jesus Christ is Lord" (Phil. 2:11); "Jesus is the Christ" (1 John 5:1); "Jesus is the Son of God" (1 John 4:15).

Accustomed to hearing these ancient terms applied only to Jesus, we cannot imagine them being used any other way. We often do not realize that these very titles were formerly used by and about political leaders. "These confessions . . . had negative connotations. That is, they were a denial of other messiahs and other lords (i.e., Caesar)."[18] Every application of such labels to Jesus was an overt rejection of other political lords, rulers, and messiahs.

While we, of course, owe some obligations to the state (Rom. 13:1), that responsibility to the authority of others comes from God alone. "For there is no authority except from God, and those that exist have been instituted by God" (Rom. 13:1b). Thus even this exhortation reveals that God is the true Lord of lords and King of kings. When there is a contest between God's higher authority and human jurisdictions, our obligation is clear: "We must obey God rather than men" (Acts 5:29).

Subversive Mysticism

One has only to study the ecstatic visions of biblical prophets to understand the political nature of God's reality. The future holds a promise that someday God's authority will be completely accomplished on earth as in heaven. Until then, we have the prophets to reveal for us what is ahead.

Micaiah was tempted to abandon his prophetic vocation when faced by two men who had control over his life. Their authority and dominion was evident. "Now the king of Israel and Jehoshaphat the king of Judah were sitting on their thrones, arrayed in their robes. . . ." (1 Kings 22:10).

But Micaiah was not intimidated. Rather, he spoke forth the deepest political reality. "Therefore hear the word of the Lord: I saw the Lord sitting on his throne, and all the host of heaven standing beside him on his right hand and on his left . . ." (1 Kings 22:19).

The succeeding verses show that God—not the finely arrayed monarchs—controls history. This illustrates God's ultimate sovereignty. God does not do the king's pleasure; the kings should serve God, the Most High King of kings.

For this reason, Isaiah did not worry about the passing away of human monarchs; he knew who truly ruled the world. "In the year that King Uzziah died I saw the Lord sitting upon a throne, high and lifted up; and his train filled the temple" (Isa. 6:1).

When God's word came to Jeremiah, that hesitant man was given an overtly political call. He was "appointed . . . a prophet to the nations" (Jer. 1:5). Likewise, Ezekiel's visions (Ezek. 1) are connected to the Ark of the Covenant, the throne of God.

Jesus predicted that someday even his enemies would be incontrovertibly faced with his majestic political authority.

Again the high priest asked him, "Are you the Christ, the Son of the Blessed?" And Jesus said, "I am; and you will see the Son of man seated at the right hand of Power, and coming with the clouds of heaven" (Mark 14:61-62).

Stephen, just before his execution, also had a political vision. "Behold, I see the heavens opened, and the Son of man standing at the right hand of God" (Acts 7:56). This was daring stuff in a day when kings often had divine pretensions and liked to play God (Acts 12:21ff.). We sometimes mistake mysticism as extremely personal, but the visions of these mystics proclaimed ultimate political realities.

This is gloriously evident in the Bible's most mysterious book, the Revelation of John. Revelation is subject to much distortion and misunderstanding. In my work as a pastor, I often meet mentally ill people who are particularly susceptible to the vivid and perplexing images found here. At such times, I might almost wish Revelation had not been included in the canon.

But not only the mentally deluded are derailed by Revelation. Most of the popular eschatological speculations miss the important thrust of Revelation, the Bible's most politically subversive and worshipful book.

One of my seminary professors only reluctantly accepted the challenge to teach this book. Many are too quick to conclude that Revelation is a bizarre anomaly in the canon. Careful study reveals that Revelation is deeply-rooted in the rest of the Bible. About 70 percent of its verses are direct references to Old Testament passages. My hesitant professor experienced a personal revelation when he finally did tackle the book. He concluded that all prophecy and indeed all Scripture is summarized and fulfilled in Revelation.

Discussions have long raged—and will rage—over the structure and meaning of Revelation. It is an issue not likely to be resolved.

Nevertheless, one thing we can say is that the rhythm of the book has at its heart acts of worship. From the beginning, John reports the vision that he had "in the Spirit on the Lord's day" (Rev. 1:10), possibly in the context of worship. The book itself was meant to be read aloud in congregations, possibly during worship services (1:3). It is filled with doxologies and awesome worship settings (for example, chapters 4 and 5). In contrast to the plagues, the Beast, and other threats, there is always the enthroned one (a political image) who is worshiped and adored. "Praise our God, all you . . . servants, you who fear him, small and great" (19:5).

This last verse reminds us that worship is profoundly political, as is the whole book (see 16:14; 17:2, 12-13, 18). The "worthy art thou" formula found in chapters 4 and 5 was often used to extol Caesars. But here the author of Revelation usurps and subverts those texts to glorify God instead, the true Ruler of all.

Similarly, the great multitude shouts, "Salvation belongs to our God who sits upon the throne, and to the Lamb!" (7:10). Yet emperors at that time liked to call themselves "saviors."

Likewise, the title "morning star" is applied to Jesus, although that was also a title for Caesar, specifically Domitian.[19] John uses explosively subversive language in dangerous and turbulent times.

The worship of John and his parishioners clearly revealed who truly is Lord. That was seditious enough to merit persecution and prosecution. His writings were highly and deliberately provocative. From the Emperor Caligula on, all Caesars were worshiped in the East.

Caligula used worship for his own political ends. He violated synagogues and tried to install his statue in the Temple of Jerusalem. Succeeding Caesars were also similarly tempted, wanting to be treated with wonder and adoration. There was even a rumor circulating that Nero would be resurrected.

Christians were one of the few groups to steadfastly oppose emperor worship. Even in the face of death, John and his parishioners held fast to the confession that Jesus—not Caesar—is Lord (2:10; 12:11). Even unto this age, such Christian claims threaten governments.

Governments often understand the political threat of Christianity better than Christians themselves. "Nor should it surprise us that during the Japanese occupation of Korea during the Second World War, Korean preachers were prohibited from preaching from Revelation."[20] Could it be that Revelation is shunted off and disregarded by so many today because we are unable to accept its radical politics?

Revelation shows that God is ultimately in control of the earth and its history (17:17). God will have the victory: "They will make war on the Lamb, and the Lamb will conquer them, for he is Lord of lords and King of kings, and those with him are called and chosen and faithful" (17:14). By the end, even kings—God's former enemies—will bring tribute to God the true Ruler (21:24-25).

Such potent fulfillment of God's purposes is pointed to, proclaimed, and in some sense already fulfilled in our worship. Our worship is a time when we prepare for the coming reality of God's kingdom. But it also enables us to live in that reality today. It is in worship that our temporal now intersects with God's eternal present. "Jesus Christ is the same yesterday and today and for ever" (Heb. 13:8). Thus the otherworldly worship of the elders in heaven impacts earthly reality: "and [thou] hast made them a kingdom and priests to our God, and they shall reign on earth" (Rev. 5:10).

Worship and the Politics of God

There are numerous definitions of worship afoot and they're not all bad. One of my seminary texts put it this way. "Fundamentally, worship is the celebrative response to what God has done, is doing, and promises to do."[21] Yet this definition does not say enough.

> Worship defined as celebration is much too broad; it does not distinguish between Christian and non-Christian celebration. Christian worship should be defined as the celebration of the rule of God as experienced in the life of the new community in Christ.[22]

Our celebration leads us into deeper commitment to the ways and purposes of God and God's kingdom. Thus when we praise and glorify God, we proclaim God King of kings and Lord of lords—not only over our own lives but over the whole universe. When we confess our sins, we acknowledge that we are accountable to God and must submit to God's will.

When we bring our offerings to God, we do so recognizing that everything belongs to God and these gifts are a small token of our loyalty and fealty to the kingdom. When we listen to Bible readings and sermons, we strive to hear God's word and directive for our lives.

Worship reminds us of the opposition between God's politics and the politics of the world. It roots us in God's priorities, rather than the "politically correct" temptations of the world. In 1957, a young nineteen-year-old Methodist preacher, Gene L. Davenport, understood the connections between God's politics and church worship.

> On a balmy February night, Race Relations Sunday, he was five minutes into his sermon from Ezekiel, talking of sin and righteousness, of bones drying in the sun. A procession of Klansmen in full

regalia began marching down the center aisle. Each one was carrying money in his hand. As the first one reached the altar and dropped his biased alms on the table, the little preacher stepped over the Communion rail to face them directly.

" 'We don't want your money,' he said. The robed and hooded men continued their planned ritual without answer. As the last one placed a dollar on the table the pastor scooped it all up, held it above his head, and tore the money to shreds."[23]

Such an action flies in the face of our modern worship of money, our most exalted value (dare we say our god?). I once wrote a magazine article that questioned a Christian organization's solicitation of money, suggesting we should avoid courting certain kinds of funding. Letters to the editor were outraged. One reported a story where a church treasurer responded to an accusation that some money was from the devil. " 'Twas before; 'taint now' " responded the treasurer. But Davenport would have none of the tainted money, even if it could be spent on race relations! (Only later did he rue the fact that he had not sent this money to the NAACP.)

The implications of worship range even further, however. Soon Davenport was called by an agent of the U.S. Secret Service in Birmingham, Alabama. The agent wanted to know whether Davenport was "preaching last Sunday night when some visitors came and made an offering to the church." Davenport was subsequently brought into the Secret Service office, required to make a report, and told to sign a transcribed copy of his testimony. Then he learned he might face a grand jury and a possible fine or prison sentence for defacing U.S. currency. Fortunately, he was never indicted.

Perhaps worship has become blasé because we do it so often. It is routine and even humdrum. We forget the radical political implications of worship. But the Bible shows that worship is subversive, informs all of life, and has implications for the rest of the world.[24]

Worship is crucial; it "must be central to the church and is in fact the foundational political structure from which the congregation involves itself in the world."[25] Liberation theologian James Cone writes extensively on how black worship is particularly meaningful within a context of racist politics.

Black worship . . . is a liberating event . . . that bears witness to God's presence in their midst. Through prayer, testimony, song, and sermon the people transcend the limitations of their immediate history and encounter the divine power, thereby creating a moment of ecstasy and joy wherein they recognize that the pain of oppression is not the last word about black life. . . . In this encounter, they are set free as children of God. To understand what this means for black people, we need only to remember that they have not known freedom in white America. Therefore, to be told, "You are free, my children" is to create indescribable joy and excitement in the people. They sing because they are free. Black worship is a celebration of freedom. . . . The people shout, moan, and cry as a testimony to the experience of God's liberating presence in their lives.[26]

Prayer, worship, and spirituality, then, are ultimately political. "Prayer is political action. It is, among other things, petitioning the king of the universe, and thereby proclaiming our true citizenship as members of a holy nation, the church, over which Jesus reigns as Lord."[27]

True biblical worship always orients us toward God's kingdom, reminding us of the now-and-coming reality of his gospel. "Therefore let us be grateful for receiving a kingdom that cannot be shaken, and thus let us offer to God acceptable worship, with reverence and awe; for our God is a consuming fire" (Heb. 12:28-29).

With all our hearts, lives, and prayers we yearn and move toward the day when the promise of Revelation is fulfilled. "Then the seventh angel blew his trumpet, and there were loud voices in heaven, saying, 'The kingdom of the world has become the kingdom of our Lord and of his Christ, and he shall reign for ever and ever" (Rev. 11:15).

On this great day, God's ruling over us and God's dwelling with us will be accomplished, the reign of God completely overlapping with God's abiding in us. "He will dwell with them . . . he will wipe away every tear . . . and death shall be no more, neither shall there be mourning nor crying nor pain any more, for the former things have passed away" (Rev. 21:3b-4).

Our worship is the place and time where we already reject the former things—and live now in the reality of God's new heaven and earth.

SIX

Mystery and Ministry

Help My Unbelief

The phone call was a complete shock. "Kevin is hospitalized and dying. We think he has AIDS, although the family has not actually said so." Later, I learned it was indeed AIDS.

Good friends were calling from Chicago with this distressing news. They and Kevin were part of the church where we used to belong. I had officiated at the wedding of Kevin and his wife only two years earlier. I well remembered that day and the union of two shy, gentle, and happy people. It was a time of holy worship and joyful celebration.

Little did we realize that the marriage would be for a mere two years. And now he lay dying. Only twenty-eight years old. His wife, in her mid-twenties, would soon be a widow and their one-year-old child fatherless (wife and child were both HIV positive and thus faced their own possible death from AIDS). Now AIDS was not just an alien disease that happened elsewhere and to other people. It was claiming the life of my friend.

Kevin did not want people to know about his condition. How lonely he must have been. His impending death was kept secret until almost the end. I was with him and his family several times in the previous year but had no idea what he was suffering. It was a reminder that many—if not all—of us carry deep, deep secrets and wounds that only the love and grace of God can touch and heal. I wished I had known and might somehow have reached out to Kevin.

Within a week of the phone call, he was dead.

I went to Chicago for the funeral, representing our family, hoping to offer a little solace, looking for answers to all the "Why's" raging through my head. Why did he die so young? Why do believers suffer? Why did all this happen? But the problems of evil and suffering are not ours alone. They weave their strands throughout the gospels and are directly linked to spirituality.

I had been meditating all week on Mark 9:2-29, the story of the transfiguration and the healing of the demoniac boy. It was the text I was going to preach on. Just after Peter's great confession, "You are the Christ" (Mark 8:29), Jesus unexpectedly explains "that the Son of man must suffer many things . . . and be killed, and after three days rise again. And he said this plainly" (8:31-32a). Jesus' close identity with suffering is developed in the transfiguration and the healing of the demoniac. This is just prior to the final journey to Jerusalem. More and more the crucifixion and passion are on Jesus' mind.

And yet the story left me perplexed and questioning. It tackles two of our deepest hungers—the desire to know God, and the need to alleviate suffering. We long to experience the reality and presence of God, just as we hope to address the problems of evil in our world. To and from Chicago I reflected on these issues and wondered how this Bible text fit into Kevin's tragedy.

> And after six days, Jesus took with him Peter and James and John, and led them up a high mountain apart by themselves; and he was transfigured before them, and his garments became glistening, intensely white, as no fuller on earth could bleach them (9:2).

The transfiguration, previewing the resurrection, shows Jesus' divine power. But shining white clothes are not just a matter of glory; they symbolize martyrdom, too. So even as we see Jesus' exaltation, the disciples are warned that he will be martyred. Glory and suffering are never far apart in the gospel.

Jesus receives astounding affirmations of his importance and authority from the Law (represented by Moses), the Prophets (represented by Elijah) and God himself. "This is my beloved Son; listen to him" (9:7). Although these are heady happenings, ecstasy never lasts long and is always ambiguous. It seldom clears up misunderstandings or resolves problems. If anything, here it seems more confusing. Why does God's beloved Son wear a martyr's white clothes? Ecstatic revelation may be helpful, but it seldom explains all.

One Christmas, my wife and I drove with a friend across the country on our way home for the holidays. On a rural road, everything was suddenly suffused with a mysteriously glowing light. It was strangely wonderful. All around us, the road, the trees, and the fields shimmered. The sky was lit up and we did not understand where this inexplicable light came from. We looked about in awe and wonder, almost dumbfounded.

But as good North Americans we were busy, in a hurry, with places to go and things to do. We did not stay. We sped on. Afterward, we agreed that it was an amazing experience, but none of us knew what had happened.

The disciples did not speed away from their mystical ecstasy, but they were not allowed to remain in it, either. Jesus brought them down the mountain, asking them to keep the transfiguration secret until after he rose from the dead. That request in itself showed that Jesus was to die.

Not surprisingly, the disciples were confused. Here Jesus had been glowing whiter than a shirt washed in All-Temperature Cheer. He had been receiving heavy-duty support from some of the heavyweights in the faith. The disciples naturally thought mystical glory had moved him—and hopefully them as well—beyond suffering once and for all.

At times we are afforded overwhelming glimpses of God's grandeur. But life is also a routine of the humdrum and mundane. Dishes, disputes, laundry, home repair, car maintenance, the lawn. Neither day-to-day work nor day-to-day worry are ever done. It is not our lot to dwell always on the transfiguration's ecstatic edge.

But not only daily duties call us back to earth. We live in a creation in turmoil. Our world is a tragic one. Pain and loss may be the biggest challenge to our faith. Jesus' glory does not call us away from grim realities, but enables us to face them.

It is no accident, then, that all three Gospel accounts of the transfiguration are followed by the story of the demoniac boy. Jesus and the disciples descend from a mountain peak of glory to the valley of human adversity and need. Kevin's tragic death drew me again into the problem of suffering, just as the demoniac boy helped teach the disciples about Jesus' relationship to sorrow. After their prayer on the mountain they are to confront pain and suffering.

A boy was desperately ill. The father explained, "He has a dumb spirit; and wherever it seizes him, it dashes him down; and he foams and grinds his teeth and becomes rigid" (Mark 9:17-18). The spirit "often cast him into the fire and into water, to destroy him" (9:22).

The father could do nothing for his son. In desperation, he went to Jesus. But Jesus was off at a mountaintop retreat. The remaining disciples wanted to help, but could not.

How often I have identified with the disciples' impotence when facing problems too big for me, problems only solvable by God. The Chicago visit was an occasion for many memories. One Thanksgiving our parish put together food baskets for the poor. We sought to help people who did not know where their next meal was coming from. We set them up for a few meals, but then what? We tried not to think about it.

A local kid, a typical teenager, helped out. Involved with gangs and drugs, he was already a father and participated in some church activities. We drove around the neighborhood together, dropping off baskets and seeing where people lived. We saw a *barrio* torn by poverty and violence and homes not fit to live in. We met an amputee, who had no immigration papers, and wondered what he could do to survive.

The teenager gave me pointers on the different gangs. We studied the hapless young men clustered on street corners. The biggest impact they could hope to make on the world was to form gangs, scrawl graffiti on walls, and threaten innocent lives. We returned to the church and encountered one of the sad fruits of their work.

Dolores, a parishioner, brought a friend, Olivia. We had heard of Olivia's family because her fifteen-year-old son was gunned down two blocks from the church a few days earlier. He was coming out of a taco stand when some gang kids did their deed. He was buried the very day that she visited us; it would have been his birthday. He perished on November 23, her husband's birthday, except that her husband had died several years before of leukemia.

This woman grieved bitterly about too many lives lost too early. I tried to share her grief by telling her that my only sibling, my sister, died at seventeen. Her response chilled me. "Was she killed?" she asked. No, my sister had also died of leukemia.

How could I minister to Olivia? Her despair was even deeper than that of the demoniac's father. I was contentedly working on food baskets. I had never been hungry. I had my beautiful baby daughter by my side. She would have her first birthday the very next day. What could I say? "Someday we will have a birthday party for your husband, your son, my sister, and my daughter in heaven. . . . Someday." But what about now?

Just so were the disciples stymied by the demoniac's insurmountable problems.

> When Jesus returned from the mountain, the father begged and pleaded: ". . . if you can do anything, have pity on us and help us."
> Jesus replied: "If you can! All things are possible to him who believes" (9:22-23).

The man had neither time nor energy for theological discussions. "Immediately the father of the child cried out and said, 'I believe; help my unbelief!'" (9:24)

This is not only the cry of the troubled and suffering father. It is also that of the disciples. His aching echoed their struggles. They believed in Jesus, believed in the Christ, but why did he keep talking about death and the cross?

Surely he of all people could bring them immediately into a glorious tear-free existence! They had seen his glory on the mountain. Why did they have to descend into the valley of suffering? And why turn their faces toward the dangerous city of Jerusalem?

They had been to the mountaintop and wanted to stay there.

While Jesus talked about the cross, they wanted glory, success, and prestige. Faced with suffering and tragedy, they were stymied and impotent, unable to act. Completely useless. "I believe; help my unbelief!"

This is not only the voice of a troubled father and confused disciples. It is our voice, yours and mine. "Lord, I believe; help my unbelief!" This is our cry, our appeal. "Lord, you touched us. You healed us, recreated us, and made us alive. We have felt you in so many places. But there are gaps, holes, and questions. So much is left unanswered. We don't always feel you or know you. Would that we did! Would that we could always carry the assurance of the transfiguration with us. But our spirits are too often deaf and dumb like the spirit of that troubled lad."

In the weeks just prior to the Chicago funeral, three people who did not know each other told me the same thing. "I open the Bible and try to read, but there's nothing that makes sense to me." I thought of them as I reflected on the demoniac's father.

Soon Kevin's mother also reminded me of this father as she buried her son, wailing by the grave in a heart-piercing cry of despair. Many of us maintained our composure until that very moment. But we could no longer hold back the tears when we heard the grieving mother. Parents burying their children is one of the saddest tragedies in life.

The father reminded me of myself, too. I went to the funeral as a gesture of sympathy, solidarity, and support. But I also went seeking and searching, hoping for an answer. I wanted relief for the latest hole in my heart. "I believe, help my unbelief!"

At the service in our former church, I prayed with friends and former neighbors. And I listened to a marvelous sermon. I did not find answers, but I found reminders and signs and some small comfort. During the service, between familiar prayer-drenched walls where God first called me to be a pastor, I heard God nudge me again.

Later, by the grave, with the cold Chicago winter wind biting into our necks, we huddled together for warmth and I remembered how God works through the company of others. This was reinforced when we returned to the church for a dose of potluck lunch therapy. Fellowship eased the grief a little.

Through it all, I thought about this gospel story and finally began to understand. In the transfiguration, Jesus reminded the disciples of what was ahead, the glory of the resurrection. But that is no easy route. Jesus warned of the suffering and the cross which must come first. It would be horrible, but it would not be the end.

Death is awful and often seems unfair. However (and this we have on faith), it is not the end of life. "Truly, truly, I say to you, unless a grain of wheat falls into the earth and dies, it remains alone; but if it dies, it bears much fruit" (John 12:24). Does that make death easy? Most assuredly not. Does it answer all our painful questions? Of course not.

Jesus healed the possessed boy. But even healing can be terrible. "And after crying out and convulsing him terribly, [the deaf and dumb spirit] came out, and the boy was like a corpse; so that most of them said, 'He is dead'" (9:26).

By now perhaps the father regretted ever speaking to Jesus. "But Jesus took [the boy] by the hand and lifted him up, and he arose" (9:27). The word *arose* here is the same one Mark later uses to describe Jesus' resurrection. Both the transfiguration and the healing dramatically foreshadow what lies beyond pain and suffering.

If death is the final reality, we are left without hope. Many young people in West Germany despair because of the nuclear weapons in their country. They refuse to marry, believing there is no point contributing to a world that will soon end. They do not want children, because they cannot bear the threat of watching their offspring die. A common graffiti slogan painted on house walls reads, "No future."

Jesus points beyond death to an age when no one will be sick, ailing, dying, or murdered. He invites us to embody the resurrection today, to start making this real for others. He calls us to keep looking toward that, even as we struggle through the mire of our earthly suffering.

Jesus calls us to be a transfigured community of the resurrection. Not everything ahead will be easy. Martin Luther King, Jr., spoke of being to the mountaintop the night before he was assassinated. And that assurance enabled him to face his martyrdom.

God is with us and for us. God suffers and cries along with us. Jesus preceded us through death.

> Christianity . . . ultimately offers no theoretical solution at all. It merely points to the cross and says that, practically speaking, there is no evil so dark and so obscene—not even this—but that God can turn it to good.[1]

We are called to be a community of love and support for those in pain and mourning, where wounds can be healed and brokenness mended. In solidarity with the Chicago parish, I found comfort. And so our spirituality leads us into the heart of the world's pain, enables us to bring healing, and points us beyond pain to the reality of the resurrection. God's mysteries empower our ministries.

At my former church, I remembered the compelling words of one of its services. "We proclaim Jesus Christ, crucified and risen, our Judge and our Hope. In life, in death, in life beyond death, God is with us. We are not alone. Thanks be to God!" Amen!

Introduction
to Part Two

It is now evident that spirituality has diverse political implications. Without justice and compassion (embracing God's kingdom and participating in its growth), spirituality is idolatry. This certainly confirms a suspicion of many social activists—religious rituals are not ends in and of themselves. But some people go to the opposite extreme, believing that spiritual disciplines are of little or no value to the building of God's kingdom. This view suggests that all that matters is doing, accomplishing, and being effective. But this need not be our conclusion.

Now that we have explored the biblical understanding and base of spirituality, we are able to consider and test further understandings. We are the happy beneficiaries of long traditions of Christian spirituality. A mystical strand has long weaved its warp through our faith. Not surprisingly, a contemplative suspicion can also be confirmed—spiritual disciplines are integrally related to lives of justice and love. Indeed spirituality is vital to building God's kingdom. In fact, kingdom workers are in special need of spirituality. It is not enough to claim to be busy for God.

You often hear the advice that if you keep busy, it will be over before you know it, and the tragedy of it is that it is true. Life is busy. It comes at you like a great wave, and if you handle things right, you manage to keep your head above water and go tearing along with it, but if you are not careful, you get pulled under and rolled to the point where you no longer know who you are or where you are going.[1]

Being busy does not absolve us from the responsibility to pray. Rather, the demands of kingdom work increase the need for prayer.

Spirituality depends entirely on God's grace. It is not within human control and manipulation. It cannot be created when convenient or only when one has the urge. Rather, without God's loving initiative toward us, we would be alone. This does not exclude the importance of human participation in the process. Some tend to be one-sided and one-tracked, believing that everything must be a contest between two opposites where only one side is right. But in spirituality, truths are often in dynamic tension with one another.

Spirituality is here understood as primarily interaction with God. Interaction implies a living relationship between at least two partners. It is active as well as passive. As relationship rather than science, it is not subject to rigorous analysis. It must be lived out and may be reflected upon.

It is in life that we interact with God. We are addressed by God in life, and it is also in life that we address God. Thus we need to be open to God. Without such openness, we will not know God and not be able to grow in needed love and compassion for the world. We will be self-centered, rather than other-directed.

Openness to God is dangerous, because we do not know where it will lead. But it is essential for our lifelong conversion. In this openness to God we begin to understand Paul's call to ceaseless prayer. We are open to God and listen to God in all aspects of our lives. All that we do can lead to deeper communion with God. We know that God's presence pervades the whole of our lives. By being aware of God's dwelling and abiding even (and especially) in the nitty-gritty, our ministry reveals God's presence in the world.

Our ministry is integrally bound up with our spirituality. One does not exist without the other. There are many ways to understand this. Much in spirituality has specific relevance for the building of God's kingdom. Spirituality helps us understand the importance of ends and means. All people and activities are ends, not means. We do not value people for their productivity. We value them because God values them. We do not indulge in actions merely because they may appear effective. We do what God calls us to.

Further, those busy on God's behalf particularly need the confessional aspect of spirituality. Without it, we are prone to self-righteousness. We will not be Christlike in our ministry. The fruits of spirituality, specifically hope and compassion, help us in our work. Without either, ministry would not reflect Christ's kingdom. Lives without compassion and hope do not bear the fruit of God's kingdom. Nevertheless, these fruits are merely tests of spirituality, not the basis for its worth.

Thus it is clear that spirituality has numerous important implications for the ministry of God's kingdom builder. Not only is it without biblical foundation if it is not just and compassionate, but being just and loving is rooted in spirituality.

SEVEN

Basics of Spirituality

One winter day while working in the church office, I read a magnificent little account of an event during Frederick Buechner's teaching career. He describes entering his classroom on a winter afternoon during the beginning of a promising sunset. He was going to teach as usual when the impulse came to turn off the lights.

> The room faced west so as soon as it went dark, everything disappeared except what we could see through the windows, and there it was—the entire sky on fire by then, like the end of the world or the beginning of the world. You might think that somebody would have said something. Teachers do not usually plunge their students into that kind of darkness, and you might have expected a wisecrack or two, or at least the creaking of chairs as people turned around to see if the old bird had finally lost his mind. But the astonishing thing was that the silence was as complete as you can get it in a room full of people, and we all sat there unmoving for as long as it took the extraordinary spectacle to fade slowly away.[1]

The splendidly rich silence lasted no less than twenty minutes. "We just sat there in the near-dark and watched one day of our lives come to an end, and it is no immodesty to say that it was a great class because my only contribution was to snap off the lights and then hold my tongue."[2]

I was moved by Buechner's description. It reminded me of

luminous moments of silence in my own life. It stirred recollections of classes that I have taught which went well without my planning or organization. I also thought that it had been a long while since I watched either a sunset or a sunrise.

I drifted out of my reflective reverie and realized that my office hours were finished and my work done. I thought more about the story as I shut down the office. I strolled through the cold January air to my car. *That is a good story*, I thought. All around me, the trees were thickly coated with snow.

As I pulled out of the church alley onto the street, I looked east and west to see whether it was safe to move onto the street. I saw that the sky was on fire with the setting sun. It seemed especially profound since I had just been moved by a description of a sunset. I remembered again that I had not admired a sunset in a long while. But I am a busy, purposeful (or is that driven?) man. I pushed the gear shift into place and moved on.

I drove a short block east and then turned north, facing Detroit's magnificent skyline. Although the direct sunlight was blocked by houses to my left, Detroit's skyscrapers were aglow with fiery reflections. And each time I passed through an intersection, the sunset's brightness slapped me on the left side of the face.

Even so, after about a mile my thoughts were elsewhere. I came to an intersection and turned east. Now I could not even look in the rearview mirror because of the setting's sun's bright reflection. I could not see behind me, but I could feel the sun beaming its beautiful rays on me. Try as I would that afternoon, I could not avoid the sun.

In my experience, God pursues us with the same tenaciousness as that glorious sunset. God is also an aggressive initiator. God does not let us go, but chases, calls, and woos us. God reveals divine beauty and tries to attract us to it. But we find it so easy to ignore God and God's great glory.

Elsewhere, Buechner notes just one of the little signs that point us to God, a sign all too easy to ignore.

Every automobile bears on its license plate a number which represents the number of years that have elapsed since the birth of

Christ. This is a powerful symbol of the ubiquity of God and the indifference of man.[3]

Rhythms, not Dichotomies

Prayer and spiritual disciplines are mysterious paradoxes. Ellul writes about the apparent absurdity of prayer.

> . . . the thought arises: Your Father knows what you need. Of what use is it, then, to confide our fears and plans to him, to present our requests and problems? God knows well in advance that we are not aware of all our needs, of all that saddens us, of all that lacerates us. He knows in advance. What good is it, then, to seek his blessing, his help, the gift of his Spirit?[4]

We deal here in rhythms and dialectic that are not solvable or even resolvable. Too often Christians analyze truths by breaking them into either-or's. (Just as social conflicts are reduced to the litmus test, "Whose side are you on?") Then they demand that other believers choose which side of the rhythm is a greater priority. Kingdom future or present. Spiritual or material/secular. Heaven or earth. Contemplative or active. Personal or corporate salvation. Individual or systemic ethics. Evangelism or social action. Grace or discipleship. Pastor or prophet. Private or public.

Yet these are dangerous and limited ways of examining the issues at hand. It is true, of course, that some concepts are distinguishable. But a discernible difference does not mean that the phenomena are completely separate, let alone mutually exclusive. Rather, they may be different dimensions of the same reality.

One flips a coin and sees only a head or tail facing up. Yet that does not mean that only the observable side is real or important. The one does not exist without the other. They are interdependent and both important.

The same holds true here. When we look at optical illusions, we see only one perspective at a time. Yet both are true and dependent on each other. In the same way, contemplative spirituality and kingdom work belong together; they are two facets of our one faith.

In the creation stories, one sees that dichotomies between spiritual and secular were false and even irrelevant. The condition of creation was one of harmony, shalom, and unity. There was no split between secular and sacred. Man and woman tended the Garden and communed with God. It was only after their disobedience that they experienced alienation from God. "And they heard . . . the Lord God walking in the garden . . . and . . . hid themselves from the presence of the Lord God among the trees of the garden" (Gen. 3:8). They actively avoided God's presence. Ever since, contemplatives have longed to return to Eden.

Because we fell away from our original state of close harmony with God, we consciously need to think and talk about prayer. It is often a matter of exertion and struggle. Before, our relation with God came spontaneously, without constraint or effort. "If there were oneness between God and the world, there would be no prayer. The relationship of prayer is already evidence of the lack of that oneness, which is confirmed by the fact that prayer is a combat."[5] Without our fallenness, prayer would happen naturally. Prayer, then, is that process (sometimes a struggle) by which we move with God's help into closer relationship with God.

Lord, Teach Us to Pray

It is only by God's initiative and grace that we can even begin to consider spirituality, let alone grow in it. Just as we have no control over the advent of glorious sunsets, so God's approach to us is beyond our manipulations and choices.

> For my thoughts are not your thoughts,
> neither are your ways my ways, says the Lord.
> For as the heavens are higher than the earth,
> so are my ways higher than your ways
> and my thoughts than your thoughts (Isa. 55:8-9).

On our own, we cannot reach God. God—the lofty and unattainable one—spoke to us first.

It was by God's word that we were created (Gen. 1:26). God first calls us; the original choice is not ours. Prayer is not earned. It is given to us by God. "We are forced to the conclusion that prayer is a gift from God, and that its reality depends upon him alone."[6]

Whatever means we choose to move deeper in our love for God, we know that God's first love for us is primary. "Let a man, humanly speaking, love God in the uprightness of his heart—alas, God has nevertheless loved him first, God is an eternity previous—man is that far behind."[7] The familiar words of John's must never be forgotten. "We love, because he first loved us" (1 John 4:19). "Prayer is everywhere and always answering speech."[8]

Paul explains that even our prayers are somehow not actually our doing. Without God's help, we would be unable to pray. "Therefore I want you to understand that no one . . . can say 'Jesus is Lord' except by the Holy Spirit" (1 Cor. 12:3). This is an astonishing claim. "Likewise the Spirit helps us in our weakness; for we do not know how to pray as we ought, but the Spirit himself intercedes for us with sighs too deep for words" (Rom. 8:26). Without God's help, we cannot pray at all.

Simone Weil was brought up as a nonbelieving Jew in France during the first part of this century. She eventually became a Christian and describes her spiritual pilgrimage in *Waiting for God*. She notes that she prayed before she understood what she was doing. This surprised her. "I had never foreseen the possibility of . . . a real contact, person to person, here below, between a human being and God."[9] Yet God came and changed her life.

Prayer and spirituality rely on disciplines, but not all disciplines are helpful or for everyone. Nevertheless, there always remains a need for some kind of discipline. Whenever we search for guidelines and helps on prayer life, we encounter this intrinsic requirement.

> A spiritual life without discipline is impossible. Discipline is the other side of discipleship. The practice of a spiritual discipline makes us more sensitive to the small, gentle voice of God. . . . Through the practice of a spiritual discipline we become attentive to that small voice and willing to respond when we hear it.[10]

There is no satisfactory resolution to the mysterious tension between God's gracious initiative and the need for human discipline. Obviously, spiritual disciplines would be totally fruitless if God did not first reach out to us. God, of course, often breaks into places and hearts which neither anticipated nor wanted this. God does not wait for or require a disciplined human life before making the divine presence felt. But even after miraculous conversions, discipline is required in the ongoing encounter between God and human, just as God's grace is first required for that encounter.

God's grace is the more important element, of course, because it is first and is the foundation of our spirituality—just as the sunset was a gift to me. But our disciplined response is crucial if the relationship is to be growing and ongoing. "The paradox of prayer is that we have to learn how to pray while we can only receive it as a gift."[11] Again, as in the gift of the sunset, I could not enjoy and appreciate its graceful beauty unless I was prepared to set aside some time and discipline to do just that.

With the disciples, we do well to ask Jesus, "Lord, teach us to pray" (Luke 11:1). In the final analysis, we must confess that without God we are unable to pray, without God we do not know how to pray, without God we cannot pray, without God we will not know how to pray, without God we cannot learn how to pray. Paradoxically, then, it is God who must teach us how to pray to God.

God's Incarnation

The incarnation of God (God coming in the flesh) is one of the most important foundations of biblical spirituality. Certain church traditions emphasize the incarnation even more than the crucifixion-resurrection.

Earlier, we considered some biblical insights about God's incarnation. There we saw God active in (and even living in) human history. Christian activity, Christian spirituality, and indeed all Christian life, is intrinsically related to the reality of God incarnate. Jesus, who "did not count equality with God a thing to be grasped, but emptied himself" (Phil. 2:6-7) is the ultimate example of the unity and interaction of divinity and humanity.

Intriguingly, Paul mentions this as an example and exhortation to us. "Let each of you look not only to his own interest, but also to the interests of others. Have this mind among yourselves, which is yours in Christ Jesus" (Phil. 2:4-5). Spirituality aims to help us grow in this "mind of Jesus."

John provides a beautiful description of the incarnation: "And the Word became flesh and dwelt among us, full of grace and truth; we have beheld his glory, glory as of the only Son from the Father" (John 1:14). The Word came in concrete bodily form. Elsewhere, John points out that this reality was one that "we have seen with our eyes, which we have looked upon and touched with our hands" (1 John 1:1).

Prayer, although a struggle and a combat, is an intrinsic part of who we originally are. It partly involves a move inward because God is near and also speaks to us from within. We are surrounded by so many diversions and distractions that we usually are not aware of God's nearness. But God is patient, as God's incarnation proves. Kierkegaard writes, "He went, in sooth, the infinitely long way from being God to becoming man, and that way He went in search of sinners."[12] Thus we are left with a strange paradox: God acting on us to renew the divine image within us.

Our disciplined life of prayer becomes another opportunity for God to make real his kingdom on earth.

Interaction with God

There are many different ways to understand spirituality. *Spirit*, *spirituality*, and *spiritual formation* are all terms that are hard to grasp. They are elusive, beyond our control or understanding. "The wind blows where it wills . . . but you do not know whence it comes or whither it goes; so it is with every one who is born of the Spirit" (John 3:8). There can be no precise or exact words here.

Thus we hear many varying explanations. Unfortunately, much of what is written about prayer and spirituality is unnecessarily complicated and mysterious. While we cannot hope to understand or control God, we can be sure that God is eager to be in relationship with us.

Come to me, all who labor and are heavy laden, and I will give you rest. Take my yoke upon you, and learn from me; for I am gentle and

lowly in heart, and you will find rest for your souls. For my yoke is
easy, and my burden is light (Matt. 11:28-30).

Here we understand spirituality as interaction with God. That
is admittedly a broad definition. Interaction, like relationship,
embraces many activities and ideas, including listening, talking,
being present with, playing, celebration, mourning, activity,
living. Our spirituality, our relationship with God, our interaction with God affects all of our lives, not only what we do before
meals or as we prepare for sleep. An early Church Father, Cle-
ment of Alexandria, said that "prayer is keeping company with
God."

By describing spirituality as interaction, we reckon with the
truth that spirituality has both inner and outer sides. The inner
side of interaction is our attitudes and emotions toward God.
While we can hide this from others, God knows us from within.
"For the Lord sees not as [a human] sees; [a human] looks on
the outward appearance, but the Lord looks on the heart" (1
Sam. 16:7).

The outer side of our interaction is the practical things we do
that reflect our relationship with God. "True worship of God
consists quite simply in doing God's will."[13] Anabaptists have always believed that knowing God involves discipleship, following Jesus. Thus we often quote Hans Denck, "No one knows
Christ truly, except he follows him in life."

We have seen that our relationship is two-sided in another
way. In some respects it is intentional—God awaits our conscious and deliberate response to his initiative. On the other
hand, our relationship is unintentional—God initiated it with us
even before we were interested in relating to God, as God did
with Simone Weil.

Describing spirituality as interaction lets us see that it is an
ongoing and dynamic relationship, with give-and-take from
both sides. With such a description, we remember that service
and interacting with people is part of our spirituality, our
relationship with God.

Furthermore, this description of spirituality as interaction
reminds us that all people relate to God. Ignoring God, rebelling
against God, or committing idolatry are all forms of relating to

God. Thus all people everywhere practice some form of spirituality. In fact, the whole of our lives are a form of spirituality. Whatever preoccupies us, whatever we spend our time, energy, and money on, whatever we center our life around, reveals our spirituality.

The issue, then, is not whether or not we practice spirituality. Everyone does. The question is whether or not we are spiritual in ways that God has initiated and recommended. (We previously saw that much of what passes for spiritual disciplines is often idolatrous.)

Spirituality is not subject to scientific analysis. It is full of mysteries and paradoxes. It cannot be charted or tabulated. Thus we seek to explore spirituality together, but we cannot legislate for one another. God may call one person to certain disciplines and devotions, but that does not mean that everyone is called to them. What we can be sure of is that God seeks a uniquely intimate relationship with each person.

The goal of Christian spirituality is to live at all times in the presence of God, keeping God's company and paying attention to God. By so doing, we are conscious of our interaction and involvement with God at all times, all levels, and in all places. Our lives are continually faced with these questions: Will we walk with God or will we walk on our own? Will we lead lives of selfishness and conceit? Or will we love God, love others, and love ourselves?

EIGHT

Keeping Company with God

Listening to God in Life

Since spirituality is interaction with God, it is a relationship, our most important relationship. A crucial part of any healthy relationship is listening. There are many ways of listening to God, and we consider a few here.

One essential way to hear God is simply to pay attention to God. How does God speak to us? When we look around, do we see manifestations of God's kingdom and healing? Do certain people around us reveal or reflect Jesus' spirit? Do particular Bible texts grip us and seem especially meaningful?

It is crucial that we always keep our ears open to God. God has a hand in the shape and direction of our lives. Our God is revealed in history and often speaks to us through the events of our lives. By careful discernment and disciplined awareness, we can hear God address us. This is a lifelong pursuit.

One need not go to a monastery, jail cell, closet, or desert to learn this discipline. While places of retreat and separation are helpful and sometimes even essential, we need to learn how to live in God's presence in all places and at all times. We cannot wait for "right" moment. Living in God's presence even when circumstances perplex and overwhelm us is a great gift.

I appreciate occasional opportunities for retreat. If time permits, I generally go to a monastery for a few days. My visits there are usually helpful and encouraging. When I am particularly stressed, I think, *How nice it would be to live here all year. To walk in the woods, to pray, to read, and to have no responsibilities.*

But my retreats are not taken to make the rest of my life seem shabby. Rather, retreats are oases, shelters, and feasts meant to enrich the whole of my life. The immediate purpose of a retreat is to settle down, be centered, and listen to God at that particular stage of life. Sometimes retreats help me process recent events; sometimes they aid me in making important decisions.

But retreats have longer range significance. They are most worthwhile when they inform my whole life. I especially appreciate my retreats as they teach me to pray, not only in the woods or the monastery, but also in the hurly-burly of home and work.

We have seen that our God is God-with-us, God-in-the-flesh, God-in-history. This means we can expect to see God at work around us, with us, and within us. With the villagers of Nain we can proclaim, "God has visited his people!" (Luke 7:16).

So often, we only notice God when things go wrong. Then we are quick to complain or ask God to change things. Then we sometimes blame God for unfortunate circumstances. But we are much slower to give God credit for all the blessings, mercies, and graces in our lives.

Paul advises, "Rejoice in the Lord always; again I will say, Rejoice" (Phil. 4:4). Elsewhere, he writes, "Rejoice always, pray constantly, give thanks in all circumstances; for this is the will of God in Christ Jesus for you" (1 Thess. 5:16-18). But this seems to be against our nature.

Dreams Deferred and the Mystery of the Doors

As a pastor, I often have the privilege of hearing what most troubles and hurts people. People tell me their stories, which invariably include the moments of their greatest pain. "Why did God let this happen?" Or worse, "Why did God do this to me?" many lament.

I do not know the answers. I do what I can, sharing their grief and praying with and for them. I have no doubt God feels pain with us. But that is not always comforting knowledge. In moments of pain, we just want the pain to go away, not be spread around. Besides, if God feels the pain, why not just take it away?

But when we only look at the negative side of our lives, we miss half the picture. We tend to notice God only when things do not go our way. How often, as people share their life stories, I am amazed by the gracious ways that God has reached out to them, healed them, and yes, even saved them. I hear many stories of God's miraculous interventions. I certainly know that God has gone to great lengths to reach out to me, care for me, and call me. Yet we are so slow to praise God and give thanks for the manifold ways God works in our lives.

Sometimes it is difficult to understand what God is doing. In 2 Samuel 7, David ran into a problem when he desired to do something for God. In spite of his noble aspirations, he was turned down flat by God. This made no sense to him.

David was highly successful as Israel's king. His reign was a time of unparalleled security for the nation. Such prosperity would never be attained again. He had a beautiful palace built for himself. For a variety of reasons, he did not settle for just his own palace but decided he would also build God a special home, a temple. Until then, Israel's main shrine was the Tabernacle, a mere tent. David the class-conscious king knew that only lowly nomads lived in tents. Surely God deserved better.

David had a deeply loving relationship with God. Thus his thoughts turned to God. Yet God refused the plan. David was not crushed by this, however, because the rejection also contained good news and marvelous promises. "I will make for you a great name, like the name of the great ones of the earth" (2 Sam. 7:9b). Not surprisingly, David accepted the offer.

It is difficult to discern and understand the ways of God. David thought he was doing God's will, but God opposed him. I find that Christians often speak very casually about God's will. Sometimes we too quickly conclude that something is or is not God's will. We need to learn to trust God with the bigger picture.

Sometimes we are too simplistic in our analysis of God's work. Several years ago, Lorna and I were catching up with a longtime friend. He was trying to make decisions about his future. He had just lost a housemate, but someone else had expressed interest in sharing his home. At the same time, he had a job offer that would entail moving to another city. Decisions, decisions.

"But you know," he said, "I just can't understand why God would give me a housemate here and offer me a job elsewhere."

My friend's theology suggested that God has clearly mapped out all the specifics of our life. If we just know how to read God's signs, we will make no mistakes. Thus we never have to make decisions or choices. God will always close the wrong doors and open the right ones, one at a time, in front of us.

Now it is true, of course, that the Bible occasionally uses language about "open doors," but this hardly means that all of our decisions should be made on this basis. Sometimes God will want us to avoid open doors. Sometimes God wants us to overcome and force open closed doors.

As it happens, the day before this frustrating conversation with our friend, I had a frightening experience of doors being carefully controlled and manipulated by a higher force. I went to visit another friend. As I approached his home, I came to a fence that was thirty feet high and topped with nasty looking rolls of barbed wire.

Once my i.d. met the guard's approval, a tall fence door was opened by some unseen person's hand. I entered the door; it closed firmly behind me. But then another locked door faced me.

Caught between two doors. No choices but to wait and hope. All I could do was stand there until the next door opened. During my visit, I had to pass through several sets of double doors securely locked behind and before me.

It is a harrowing experience to have one door lock behind you and be completely at the mercy of someone else to open the next. That is how my friend believes that God operates, like the warden of a maximum security prison.

But our life is not like that. God does not open and close one door after another at God's own inexplicable pace, leaving us no room or freedom for decisions. Generally, we are faced with many doors and many choices all at once. Some are open and some are closed.

Some open doors are temptations. When Jesus was in the desert, Satan offered three temptations, in effect three open doors. Jesus rejected them all. Visiting New Orleans, I was shocked to notice that the sleaziest bars had their doors thrown wide open, so that people on the street could gawk at the unseemly activities within and hopefully be lured inside. Those doors were not opportunities, but temptations.

All too often, language about "open doors" (or language about "laying out the fleece") is just an excuse to do what we want or to avoid making a hard decision. Once, a group of women were in a Bible study together, discussing decisions about the spending of money.

One woman said, "Sometimes when I'm shopping I see something really nice that I'd like to have, a pretty piece of clothing or some nice jewelry. When I'm not sure whether or not to indulge, then I say a little prayer to God asking for his advice. Then I go away for an hour. When I come back, if it's still there, I assume it's an open door from God and I may buy it. So I do."

While one can of course commend any person's reliance on God during economic decisions, this process is suspect. What is so holy about a one-hour wait? Why not select a duration of several days or weeks or months? How often does a single item just disappear from a store in such a limited time? (There is usually a backup stock of items.)

This is an abuse of "open door" ideas and just an excuse to do what one really wants to do anyway. A better policy would be, if in doubt about the purchase, go to a soup kitchen and ask God how you should spend that extra money.

Several years ago, I had an amusing discussion about open and closed doors. I needed to make decisions about certain travel plans and whether or not I would fly. The issue involved stewardship questions of time, dollars, and energy.

To help my discernment, I made myself accountable to a respected friend in our church small group. We arbitrarily decided I would fly if I could get on a budget flight. "I would look at it as the Lord opening a door for you," she encouraged me. Such vocabulary was quite normal in our church, although I did not use it.

Later, I was speaking to another person from that church. I said quite plainly that if I found a budget flight I would go, otherwise I would stay. He was not impressed. "Interesting . . . even if indecisive."

There is at least one other problem with "open door" decisions. Some doors are closed against the gospel. Sometimes doors are barricaded against the work of God's kingdom. We seek in such situations to find faithful ways of overcoming barriers. We faithfully persist in trying to do God's will and work, in spite of obstacles and closed doors before us. Sometimes, the work of the gospel involves destruction and overcoming of closed doors. "For he is our peace, who has made us both one, and has broken down the dividing wall of hostility . . ." (Eph. 2:14).

We, like David, are people of the promise. We can live within the security of God's covenant. We do what we can, we try and do our best, of course. But beyond that, we can also relax in the mercy, care, and providence of God. We do not always know what is ahead or understand what is happening. "We walk by faith, not by sight" (2 Cor. 5:7).

The Christian faith is not as secure as a stay in a maximum security prison where all the doors are ominously opened and closed for us, one at a time. God moves with us in mysterious and unpredictable ways, in a dance that we often cannot recognize until long after the fact.

Once, Lorna and I were on the train traveling toward Windsor. There were only a few seats, so the conductor directed us to sit with a stranger. I did not feel like talking to anyone, but noticed that my neighbor was reading a book by one of my favorite authors. We began to talk. He, a Christian, was a former priest and we had friends in common in my old Chicago neighborhood. In his ministry as a priest, he had experienced a nervous breakdown and left the profession. He applied at a restaurant to be a waiter, since he no longer felt able to perform his calling. But there was no job opening.

The owner, however, recognized my new friend as a former priest. He noted that he needed a piano player in the bar. The priest had never done such work. He had never even been in a bar before. He went home and considered the offer. He had no money, no income, no job, and his rent was due. He took the job.

Mysteriously it developed into other things. He eventually became a professional musician and earned his money from his music. Mentally and emotionally, he recovered from his breakdown. He is now able to minister again on God's behalf, performing concerts and leading retreats. Now some might have trouble with the kind of job that he took. Yet he has every reason to believe that through this opportunity God's grace worked.

In the light of God's providence, the *no* of the priest's breakdown became a *yes* of unexpected, grace-filled, surprising opportunities. Likewise, we too can remember how God has worked in our lives and celebrate his work in the lives of our brothers and sisters. We can rejoice in the fact that all our *no*'s and small dreams will one day be surpassed, embraced, and enveloped in God's great and loving *yes*!

The Providence of God

For thus says the Lord: When seventy years are completed for Babylon, I will visit you, and I will fulfil to you my promise and bring you back to this place. For I know the plans I have for you, says the Lord, plans for welfare and not for evil, to give you a future and a hope. Then you will call upon me and come and pray to me, and I will hear you. You will seek me and find me; when you seek me with all your heart, I will be found by you, says the Lord (Jer. 29:10-14).

God is willing to remain faithful to us even when we sin or make mistakes. God works with us even when we go astray, wandering through the wrong open doors or avoiding the right closed doors. With infinite patience, God reaches out to us and offers us support and care. We may still have to live with the consequences of our sinful actions, but God helps us work through them. God supports and cares for us.

God was lovingly involved in the history of God's people, Israel, despite continual rejection. For example, they desired a human king even though this meant rejecting God as their king (1 Sam. 8). But God did not reject or abandon them. God always stood ready to help and work with them. Even when we make mistakes and choose the wrong directions, God's arms stretch out to us.

When we talk about God's leading, God's providence, God's care, we like it when everything happens to work out nicely. Sometimes we are amazed by beautiful coincidences and astonishing serendipity. Certainly, God does work that way at times.

But God does not need everything neat and tidy to perform the divine work and purposes. (This is good news for certain relaxed members of my family and frustrating news for compulsive neatniks!) God is not even deterred by our stubbornness or our rebellion. God can and does work in and beyond and even through the messiness of life.

Some time ago, I was on retreat at a monastery. I was surprised to meet a man that I had known briefly some six years earlier. After dinner, we sat on a bench under the trees and watched the setting sun. To my surprise, I found my companion to be a wounded and needy soul. He spoke to me for an hour-and-a-half about some of the hard things going on in his life. There was little for me to say, so I tried to listen.

The next morning, I was hiking through the woods near the lake. I reveled in the smell of the trees and in the new spring growth. Carrying my binoculars, I was on the look-out for birds. Then I noticed a movement on the lake. I whipped my binoculars to my eyes and saw my friend. The breeze gently stirred the waves of water as he sat alone in a drifting rowboat. His rounded shoulders hunched over, he was poring over a prayer book, apparently trying to pray. He looked sad, lonely, and a little lost.

I knew my friend was struggling with an uncertain future. Middle-aged, he had just lost his job and had no good prospects of another. He had been laid off partly because of Christian convictions he could not keep to himself. I knew he was wrestling with hard and difficult issues. And seeing him there, sad and lonely, adrift on a lake and in life, I ached for him. But I didn't know what I could do. Except to pray for and with him.

But my mind strayed back to the conversation we had the evening before. During one long monologue, he said something that particularly caught my ear. "People no longer believe in the providence of God." We don't really believe that God works in the world. We do not trust that God can act in the world.

I was struck by the truth of his words. I realized then that I seldom, if ever, use the word *providence*. It almost sounded foreign to me. Because of this conversation, something that happened the next day seemed especially significant. I was poking through a pile of books and found one called, appropriately enough, *The Providence of God.*[1]

Now I had never heard of this book before, but obviously it caught my attention because of what my fellow retreatant had said. Otherwise, I would not have looked at it twice! As I considered it, I was further struck by the fact that it was by Georgia Harkness. I have never read anything by her, but have meant to for years. She was the favorite author of the pastor who helped me find my pastoral call.

Harkness writes:

> The providence of God means the goodness of God and His guiding, sustaining care. Belief in providence in the most general sense implies the goodness as well as the power of God in the creation, ordering, and maintaining of His world, embracing the entire world . . . . However, it is in the destinies of human individuals that belief in providence centers. Both a positive Christian faith in providence and the perplexities connected with it find their focus in God's care of the individual person.
>
> The word *providence* is derived from the Latin *pro* and *videre*, "to see ahead." By an interesting juxtaposition of English usage it means also "to look after." In a word, to believe in providence is to believe that God sees the way before us and looks after us as we seek to walk in it.[2]

I work for a small, struggling church planting. For some time, we have searched long and hard to acquire a building. We discerned and believed that such an acquisition would help our ministry. But our search was hampered by meager resources and the high cost of property.

Sometimes during this difficult process, people would say to me, "Well, if it's God's will for us to have a building, then we will get it."

Frankly, my response to this statement is mixed. It has truth of course, but there is also a dangerous fallacy embedded in it. The truth is this: God cares for us, God will care for us, God supports us, God will continue to work with us, the Lord provides. Fine.

But we must never fall into the trap of fatalism, thinking that everything that happens is exactly what God wills. A lot occurs in this world that is not God's will. We do not believe that God wills everything to happen exactly as it happens, otherwise nothing could truly be labeled evil or sin. Rather, as believers in the resurrection, we confess that God is able to work even in and through circumstances that are against the divine will.

There was one church building possibility that presented itself to us. Numerous factors convinced us that it was the building for us. The dwindling congregation there spoke no English. It was the only church in a particularly needy neighborhood, but because of language barriers it did no outreach. We negotiated for some time; it seemed that the deal would succeed. Then it suddenly fell through.

Some well-meaning church members tried to console each other this way: "Well, it wasn't God's will for us to have it."

But we do not know that; we cannot say that. We do not know what God's will was in that situation. All we knew for sure was that that congregation decided not to sell us the building. Maybe God wanted us to have the building, perhaps God urged them to sell it to us, possibly they disobeyed by clinging to their building.

In such perplexing situations, it is better to confess that God can care for us, God can provide for us, and we can trust in God. These things are true in spite of circumstances beyond our choice or understanding. This is true despite the resistance of others to God's will.

I may be more than a little sensitive to these issues because of my Calvinist upbringing. I was brought up to believe that God predetermined and predestined who would be saved and who would be damned. As a child, I was proudly grateful that God selected me as one of the chosen few and made me part of the one true denomination. I felt a little sorry for all the other poor deluded souls who attended other churches.

Calvinism, as it was interpreted by those I grew up with, had an unhealthy fatalistic attitude. People often said, "You never die before your time." But they were wrong. When someone is murdered, they die before their time. It is not God's will that someone's life be brutally ended. If we kill ourselves through foolishness or deliberation, we die before our time. Such tragedies are not God's will. Ironically, those fatalistic Calvinists also opposed risky sports (skydiving, automobile racing) because that was gambling with your life. But if you never die before your time, how can you risk your life?

I do not mean to disparage Calvinists and their convictions. In spite of my suspicions, I cherish and respect their insight that God is closely connected to all the circumstances of our lives.

Spirituality helps us carry that assurance with us in our daily lives, even as we go through life with its problems and un-expected curves. When life does not go the way we like it, we can still find encouragement in God's providence. In tough times, we need to find ways of looking to God, listening to God, feeling God's presence. We appeal to God even as we trust in God.

In spite of some ambivalence about my Calvinist up-bringing, I am still moved by what I memorized in catechism.

> That the eternal Father of our Lord Jesus Christ, who out of nothing created heaven and earth with all that is in them, who also upholds and governs them by his eternal counsel and providence, is for the sake of Christ his Son my God and my Father. I trust in him so com-pletely that I have no doubt that he will provide me with all things necessary for body and soul.[3]

I do not agree with Calvinists about the source of evil, "whatever evil [God] sends upon me in this troubled life."[4] Nevertheless I agree with their conclusions about the ultimate end of evil: "whatever evil . . . he will turn to my good, for he is able to do it, being almighty God, and is determined to do it, being a faithful Father."[5]

Seeing God's Providence in Our Lives

How has God worked in and through our lives? How has God revealed the divine will to us? Where have we seen our lives move within God's providence?

Such questions are dangerous and risky. It is easy to abuse talk of God's will. One of my favorite authors, William Stringfel-low, called that "usurping the prerogative of the Word of God." He suggested that we could not claim to know God's will. I do not entirely agree, but I appreciate the caution. Too often, Christians claim divine sanction for their own selfish interests and purposes. Thus providence is seen merely as something that meets our approval.

Archbishop Frederick Temple humorously reported this conversation:

> "My aunt was suddenly prevented from going [sic] a voyage in a ship that went down—would you call that a case of Providential interference?"
> "Can't tell: didn't know your aunt."[6]

If we refuse to define providence by our own interests, preferences, and biases, we may be open to seeing how our lives fit God's purposes. Then perhaps we will see the goodness of God working itself out in our lives and history.

Again, we must not be cocky here. Often Christians boast of what God did for them and at least implicitly suggest that the suffering of others is their own fault. Visiting a Christian who is a lifer in maximum security prison, I heard him complain, "People tell us God takes a personal interest in each one of us. And then there's genocide." His point was that we who are not victims invent tortured theological excuses to blame victims. "There's got to be a good reason why God hates you all."

We need to understand how God works in our lives. In this way, we may be able to help understand how God has moved in other lives too. E. Glenn Hinson writes:

> The longer I try to minister and observe others trying to minister, the more conscious I am that ministry has to do, above all, with helping others get in touch with the working of grace in their lives and that ministers cannot help others without being touched with the working of grace in their own lives.[7]

Hinson notes that besides the regular ministries and ordinances of the church, God works through such means as Scriptures, other persons, holy writings, and experiences.[8]

I am particularly interested in how God works through our experiences. We often judge too soon the meaning of God's will. In fact, life often puts us in the midst of situations that we do not understand. Generally, we should not quickly make bold claims about God's will and plan. Since we are not God, we do not know. Often, we just have to wait and see. Many things are only understood with waiting.

> It is wholly legitimate to see best the workings of providence after events have transpired rather than predicting them in advance. To assume to know exactly how or where God will lead involves not only arrogance and human presumption but is too often tinged with wishful thinking.[9]

Looking back on my own life, I see many crucial turning points that shaped who I am, what I believe, what I do. As I have professed Christian faith since I was a small child, I have no dramatic conversion to report. But God worked through the events of my life to convert, reorient, and turn me. I will name some of them, with the hope that they might stir your own thinking and reflections about how God has worked in your life.

The most important event in my life was the death of my only sibling, Margaret Ann, when she was seventeen and I was twenty. Margaret's death, of complications connected to her leukemia, seemed grossly unfair and horrible. This was my first and—until now—worst experience in grief and mourning. The process made me uneasy with some of the simplistic answers people offered me about God's will. It stirred my resolve to minister to the pain of others.

Then there was the chain of events that led me to join a Mennonite congregation. Most important in the process was the Mennonite pastor's insistence that I read Anabaptist history and study the peace position. At first, I resisted his recommendation. Yet when I complied, I felt myself converted to a broader and deeper understanding of the gospel. I resolved to commit myself to the social ramifications of the gospel and this had implications for the kind of occupation I would pursue.

Four-and-a-half years in Chicago's inner-city neighborhood has also shaped me. I am convinced more than ever that Christians must serve the world. I passionately long for the reality of God's new kingdom on earth as in heaven. I grieve for suffering brothers and sisters everywhere.

During this period, I also spent two brief weeks in Haiti. But during those days, it was as if my senses were especially alert and heightened, for the consequences of that time still works its way through my life.

Other events convinced me of the biblical counsel to "put not your trust in princes" (Ps. 146:3). While living in the United States, I was twice prosecuted by the government for practicing freedom of speech and living up to my faith. While I did not seek these costly prosecutions, I nevertheless fell victim to them. I felt persecuted for my faith.

In Chicago, I was overjoyed by the popular movement that swept Harold Washington into the Mayor's Office. Shortly before I left Chicago, I saw Washington's progressive coalition fall apart when he died. I realized the unreliability of politics.

Finally, my call to be a pastor has been a long and involved process. For years I had no intention of pastoring. Yet God, through a complex series of events, apparently dragged me into it. Strangely and mysteriously, I find that many of the above-cited events gifted me to be the particular pastor that I am. Thus I, for one, am convinced that God takes a personal interest in me.

Perhaps Georgia Harkness said it best.

> To trust in providence is to trust in the goodness of God, whatever happens. It does not involve belief that everything that happens will be to our liking. It does not even involve belief that everything that happens is exactly as God would have it, for it is in the very nature of evil to be at variance with God's will. To trust in providence is to believe that however dark or evil a situation may be, God is with us, and with the help of God good can come out of it.[10]

As I have elsewhere noted, in my church in Chicago we used to make this glorious profession during communion: "In life! In death! In life beyond death! God is with us! We are not alone! Thanks be to God!"

NINE

On Being
Open to God
in Life

The Kingdom Is Like . . .

The awareness of God's presence and God's involvement in our lives is not only ecstatic or mysterious. To be sure, there are people who are of a charismatic, contemplative, or mystical bent.

But many of us are a little more down-to-earth. And we can take heart from the fact that God is down-to-earth too. Jesus came in concrete form, "which we have heard, which we have seen with our eyes, which we have looked upon and touched with our hands" (1 John 1:1). Thomas the doubter was given a chance to experience Jesus in the flesh. Only then did he find himself making the great confession, "My Lord and my God!" (John 20:28).

Michel Quoist, a French Roman Catholic priest, has written a marvelously simple book, *Prayers*. In it, he pens prayer-poems about what he sees and experiences all around him. His observations are surprising and inspirational. For Quoist, all aspects of life—whether a telephone call, a blackboard, a fence, a subway, or a twenty-dollar bill—are signs of God and an opportunity for prayer.

If we knew how to look at life through God's eyes, we would see it as innumerable tokens of the love of the Creator seeking the love of his creatures. The Father has put us into the world, not to walk through it with lowered eyes, but to search for him through things, events, people.[1]

Thus Quoist writes:

If we knew how to listen to God, we would hear him speaking to us. For God does speak. He speaks in his Gospels. He also speaks through life—that new gospel to which we ourselves add a page each day.[2]

This nourishing spirituality enables us to look around and hear God always and everywhere. To grow in our relationship with God does not mean to be idle. Rather, it is to be conscious and aware. Even as we are active, we can look around and know that we are in the presence of God.

If we knew how to listen to God, if we knew how to look around us, our whole life would become prayer. For it unfolds under God's eyes and no part of it must be lived without being freely offered to him.[3]

As God is revealed to us, we begin to perceive history, the circumstances of our lives, and indeed the world around us with new eyes. It is not only special times (holy-days or sacraments), special places (churches or sanctuary), or special feelings (inner clarity or euphoria) that reveal God. As we grow, we hear God at all times. Even God's silence speaks to us. God's work, presence, judgment, invitation, and good news are constantly proclaimed, reflected, and revealed all around us.

Jesus' teachings show how to hear and perceive God's word in life. His parables show sensitivity to the down-to-earth reality of God-with-us. His little stories were about plain, ordinary events and realities that everyone could relate to—farming, house cleaning, management-labor relations. People understood his stories because they were about regular life. Jesus shows us that with our ears open we can hear God speak always. All our lives can become parables of God's kingdom.

Jesus prayed before all the important points in his ministry. Some might say that Jesus knew what was ahead and thus prayed in preparation for the coming challenge. That is possible.

However, I believe that because Jesus prayed beforehand, the real importance of those events was evident. Because he was a person of prayer, he was able to read the plain signs of normal life as pointers to God's kingdom, as parables. Because he was a person of prayer, he understood that God was working through his life. Because he was a person of prayer, he allowed God to take his life in directions that were uncomfortable and disconcerting.

Without a discipline of prayer, we are liable to be deaf to the work of God around and within us. Each event in our lives can be understood in several ways. Some read everything sociologically or psychologically. Those disciplines have their place. But as Christians we strive to understand what God is telling us. Without faith, not even miracles will convince others. They can always be explained away, reduced to some other explanation and thus dismissed. Jesus warned, "If they do not hear Moses and the prophets, neither will they be convinced if some one should rise from the dead" (Luke 16:31).

The ability to perceive and interact with God is an important conversion in our lives. It is a great moment when we in faith can profess that our lives are not just randomly without direction, but part of the providential plan of God. This great conversion is a move from feeling alienated and distracted toward being centered, whole, integrated, and hopeful.

Conversion and Openness to God

God's initiative toward us calls for our response, a response often described as conversion or repentance. The New Testament word for this is *metanoia*, which means "to turn." God calls us to a twofold turning: away from our sin, and toward God. A converted life is a life open to God. Once we have allowed God to intervene with us, to change us, to rework us, we have started a lifelong process.

We are continually tempted to fill our lives and squeeze out God. It is often too hard to wait for God. God's schedule does not match ours. So we substitute family, pride, success, or money. Soon our hearts are toughened or hardened and we forget our basic need for God. Jesus said, "Blessed are the poor in spirit, for theirs is the kingdom of heaven" (Matt. 5:3). All the Beatitudes in the Sermon on the Mount are directed to people who know their need for God.

Conversion is the first step in openness to God. By joining God's kingdom and living under Christ's lordship, we turn control of our lives over to God. Sometimes we lament this loss of control. Actually, we are then free of the forces—the powers and principalities—of this dark age.

Prayer reminds us of our primary allegiance. It shows us the direction of our lives. It guides us in our walk with God. Thus all our spiritual disciplines are helpful as they gradually affect our lives.

The process of conversion is demanding. It is easy to talk of being open to God. Those who are eloquent can speak of the beauty of this process. They are not wrong. However, openness to God means turning over all of our lives to God . . . even the innermost recesses. God's light brings healing to our dark places, but it is a healing that often hurts even as it works. We must trust it though, even as we sometimes need the most bitter medicine to cure physical ailments.

This is an ongoing process. By turning to Jesus, we turn our backs to sin and the works of darkness. In the Episcopal liturgy of baptism, the candidate is asked the following crucial decisions:

> Do you renounce Satan and all the spiritual forces of wickedness that rebel against God?
> Do you renounce the evil powers of this world which corrupt and destroy the creatures of God?
> Do you renounce all sinful desires that draw you from the love of God?[4]

New life in Jesus means turning away from and renouncing the old ways. Metanoia, repentance, conversion is not only remorse but also renewal.

God's grace informs us of our sin and helps us clear away obstacles. Often, there are weak places within that never seem to change. But as God slowly removes some of the rough spots and broken edges, we become more open to God's grace. Prayer seeks to turn us to God, to keep us turned to God, and to repeatedly turn us toward God.

But this turning to God is not necessarily comfortable. After Adam and Eve sinned, they "hid themselves from the presence of the Lord God among the trees of the garden" (Gen. 3:8). Moses found himself in God's presence, but was uncomfortable there, especially with God's call.

Isaiah's experience of God's revelation was similarly unsettling. "Woe is me! For I am lost; for I am a man of unclean lips, and I dwell in the midst of a people of unclean lips; for my eyes have seen the King, the Lord of hosts!" (Isa. 6:5). Jonah the prophet disobeyed God and "rose to flee . . . from the presence of the Lord" (Jon. 1:3a).

While we may choose to pray, we do not manufacture or create prayer. God is not forced into communion or interaction with us, just because we choose to pray. We are able to pray because God has reached out to us first. Thinking that we can manipulate God with our prayers is a magical view of prayer. The Bible rejects that (as we saw in chapter four). The most we can do is receive God's gifts. First, we can interact with God because God makes it possible. When God touches that part of us made in the divine image, then we can respond to God.

Our sinful condition hampers our ability to respond to God. We are deaf, blind, and hard-hearted. In the parable of the sower we see that many places receive the word, but they are not all fit for the seed to grow. The gospel is choked in many ways.

> And others are the ones sown among thorns; they are those who hear the word, but the cares of the world, and the delight in riches, and the desire for other things, enter in and choke the word, and it proves unfruitful (Mark 4:18-19).

But God's gracious reconciliation overcomes the obstacles within us. "But those that were sown upon the good soil are the ones who hear the word and accept it and bear fruit, thirtyfold and sixtyfold and a hundredfold" (Mark 4:20).

When Erin, my eldest, was three years old, Lorna and I went to a church meeting and left our children in the care of Liz the baby-sitter.

As we left, I gave Erin some parting advice. "Now you listen to what Liz says, Erin."

When we arrived home, Erin was sitting on the couch looking forlorn and chastened. She should have been in bed. "Did you miss us, Erin?" I asked, setting myself up for disappointment.

"No," she mumbled.

Erin was worried about a confession that she felt she needed to make. "I didn't listen to Liz."

"I'm sorry?"

"I heerd her. But I didn't listen to her. I wouldn't go to bed."

"But, Erin, I told you to listen to Liz."

"I listened to her words, but I didn't listen to her."

For a three-year-old, Erin was making a sophisticated (although not entirely convincing) distinction. While listening to someone's words may be different than listening to someone, when we asked Erin to listen we were asking her to obey.

When Paul was three, he too had to learn lessons in listening. Lorna was industriously scrubbing the kitchen floor. She warned the children not to come running through. The floor was slippery; they would inevitably bump heads and posteriors. Not two minutes later Paul came charging through, wiped out, and injured the afore-mentioned body parts. Even as she comforted him, Lorna reminded him of what she had said.

"You didn't listen, Paul."

He was mortified. "I did listen. I did."

We might find ourselves distinguishing between listening and hearing. Hearing suggests a passive receptivity; we hear certain things whether we intend to or not. But listening implies a deliberate effort to be attentive.

The Bible recommends that hearing should be followed by obedience. We must discipline ourselves so that we might not only hear God's words but listen to him as he addresses us. The consequences and stakes are much more than minor bumps and bruises. "Blessed rather are those who hear the word of God and keep it!" (Luke 11:28). Perhaps we could paraphrase this as, "Blessed are those who listen to God, and not just hear God's words."

Simplicity: The Discipline of Being Open to God

Many contemplatives have observed that poverty is closely related to prayer. Francis of Assisi, a great mystic and peacemaker, chose to be poor. It is not surprising that Jesus often recommended poverty to others. For the truth is that possessions often fill our lives in harmful ways.

As I sit in my study to pray, I am often distracted. I cannot focus but keep looking around at all my beloved books. Or if I go away on retreat, I worry about many things—my job, my house, my possessions. I am so busy thinking about what I own and what I want to control (or protect) that I am deaf to God. Spiritual poverty and material poverty are not unrelated. It is no contradiction that the Beatitudes speak of "poor in spirit" in Matthew, but only of "the poor" in Luke (Matt. 5:3; Luke 6:20).

As Christians in the Western world, we are so accustomed to our possessions and accomplishments that we forget our basic dependence on God. And our possessions also invariably make us hard-hearted toward our needy neighbor and thus toward God.

A friend has a beautiful needlepoint hanging in her kitchen. A wedding gift from her grandmother, it simply reads, "Give us this day our daily bread." Familiar words, but profound, nevertheless. For this grandmother survived hard years of hunger in the Soviet Union during the 1930s. That petition in the Lord's prayer is meaningful to the old woman. She knows that all of our lives, physical and spiritual, depend on God.

Yet those words trip lightly and easily off our tongues. Too easily. To live open to God means depending on God in all areas of our life. Thus simple living is not just an Anabaptist tradition or (more recently) a countercultural fad. Simplicity is a spiritual discipline that helps keep us focused on God.

Being open toward God is a crucial and central aspect of spirituality. It is not calling God to change things or do what we want. It is rather relinquishing all to God and continually inviting God to convert us. We stand open toward God, not knowing how God will respond or what God will demand. But we dare not fill that opening ourselves. We must wait on God to be filled by God. This process of conversion to God takes all of our lives—and beyond.

Kairos and the Presence of God

We North American Christians are so busy. Hurrying here and there for our jobs, commitments, or responsibilities. Our abundant technology is supposed to simplify our lives.

When I first acquired a computer, I was overjoyed to discover it cut much of my work time in half. What a blessing! What an opportunity!

But instead of taking the chance to spend more time with people and God, I find myself working more frantically than ever. Now that I have it, I want to accomplish two or three times as much work as I used to do. Studies show that for all our labor-saving technology, families now spend less time together than they once did.

Why is it that we are so compelled, hurried, and frantic? Why is it that in a day and age when we have power machines to do almost everything, in a time when microwaves can cook food almost instantly, we have so little time to pray? I am certain that people pray less now than they used to. Our society puts so much emphasis on doing, acting, and accomplishing. The little time we have to live (which is actually longer than previous generations) is too short and we feel driven to make the best use of it. Unfortunately, the best use is generally defined not by God but by the world.

There are at least two ways of looking at time. In our modern perception of time, we see time as something that passes quickly. A fleeting opportunity to make good and accomplish much.

But we can take a longer term perspective. God is everywhere present at once and never changes. We need to remember that God controls history and time. God's perspective is substantially different than ours. "But do not ignore this one fact, beloved, that with the Lord one day is as a thousand years" (2 Pet. 3:8).

While we live in time, God is with us but also somehow beyond time. God is, in fact, the one constant. Thus we do well to count on God to orient us in the divine perspective of time.

So teach us to number our days
that we may get a heart of wisdom (Ps. 90:12).

The world sees time as *chronos*, the Greek term for profane or ordinary, linear time. Things follow one another randomly and there is little control over them. There is no meaning in the succession. We struggle to control the chaos of chronos, to extract a little security in its midst. In chronos time, the sequence of events is impersonal and meaningless.

The biblical perspective of time, however, can be described as *kairos*. Kairos is God's full time, the time of readiness, the appropriate time. The Scripture speaks of events that occur at the right, favorable, proper time (John 7:6-8; Rom. 5:6; 1 Tim. 6:15; Titus 1:3).

When we remember this, time is neither oppression nor possession. Time is not hurried, harried, hectic, or harassing. Rather, time is personal and full of opportunities. How often we miss God's purposes because we do not pay attention. "You hypocrites! You know how to interpret the appearance of earth and sky; but why do you not know how to interpret the present time [kairos]?" (Luke 12:56). Time is meaningful. Believers live in a new, different, and richer time.

The biblical view of time, as God's full time of opportunity, has clear implications for the way we live in the world. Our salvation affects not only our ethics and life-style, but even our understanding of time. Instead of being possessed and driven by it, we are liberated in it. When we live this way, our lives and ministry manifest something different and perpetually new in the world of chronos.

We live now already in the reality of God's kingdom. Thus we see salvation occurring today. We are part of the unfolding of God's kingdom on earth. "Consequently he who really occupies himself with the eternal is never busy. To be busy means, divided and scattered . . . ."[5]

Jesus preached, "The time [kairos] is fulfilled, and the kingdom of God is at hand; repent, and believe in the gospel" (Mark 1:15). Jesus' coming to earth transformed time and the meaning of our lives. We have an ongoing opportunity to join the kingdom, to repent and believe. Believing in kairos, believing that God controls history, frees us from the desperation of lives caught in chronos.

This is closely related to peacemaking. Violence is a desperate act of people willing to do anything to make history turn out the way they see fit. Violence reveals an appalling lack of trust in God. It cannot wait for God's purposes, God's kairos. It must make the preferred results right now. When we renounce the means of violence, we relinquish power and turn control over to God. "The key to the obedience of God's people is not their effectiveness but their patience (Rev. 13:10)."[6]

I get mightily tired of those who think they are justified in trying to control history—or believe that they even can (or may) control history. This is no less the sin of many activists (who profess to be peacemakers) as it is the sin of war-makers and oppressive governments.

Some time ago, friends were organizing a demonstration. Its poster slogan boasted, "We will stop the U.S. war in Central America." While I too hope for an end to such wars, the poster was disturbing. On one level, the claim was absurd. Now, years later, those protesters have not stopped the war. At a deeper level, the truth is that causality and cause-and-effect is too difficult to sort out. If all the wars stopped, we do not know whether the demonstrators did or did not accomplish it.

Most seriously, that poster betrayed a spirit of proud and zealous arrogance. "We will stop the U.S. war in Central America." We will stop it because we are so holy. We will stop it because no one else will. We will stop it because we are so clear-sighted and effective and powerful.

But how can we expect to stop anything, especially by non-violence? Such boasts are easily twisted into recommendations. The rhetoric quickly leads to justification of all manner of means, including violence.

I am not arguing against protests, but against the motives and spirits of certain demonstrations. "We will witness against the war in Central America" is acceptable. "We will pray for an end to the war" is admirable. But effectively stopping a war is beyond our means.

"Power, success, happiness, as the world knows them, are his who will fight for them hard enough; but peace, love, joy, are only from God."[7]

Jeremiah's counsel was similar.

Thus says the Lord: "Let not the wise man glory in his wisdom, let not the mighty man glory in his might, let not the rich man glory in his riches; but let him who glories glory in this, that he understands and knows me, that I am the Lord who practice steadfast love, justice, and righteousness in the earth; for in these things I delight, says the Lord" (Jer. 9:23-24).

Our glory is in knowing God; this knowing is not separate from God's passions for love, justice, and righteousness. But this knowing is different than we ourselves striving for wisdom, might, riches, or power. The knowing enables us to live by God's priorities, even when they do not appear immediately effective.

Paul writes about some further implications of kairos.

Besides this you know what hour it is, how it is full time [kairos] now for you to wake from sleep. For salvation is nearer to us now than when we first believed; the night is far gone, the day is at hand. Let us then cast off the works of darkness and put on the armor of light (Rom. 13:11-12).

Living in the new age of God's kairos, we are freed to live according to God's purposes and without the world's neurotic anxieties. We live now in the reality of God's kingdom, the power of the resurrection. Salvation history occurs today. Our task in the world is to share this new reality with our neighbors, showing that God's kingdom exists in power and might today, and that all have the opportunity to be part of God's history.

In revealing God's kairos to the world, we need to be rooted in it ourselves, which is itself an ongoing process of transformation and conversion. Through prayer, we can come to see that all our life is touched by the care and love of God. "For his steadfast love endures for ever," as Psalm 136 repeats twenty-six times.

Prayer, then, is not a way to escape life. It is a way of coming in touch with the deepest reality of life, God's involvement in it. Prayer is a means of being aware of God's presence in our lives and being assured that God's purposes undergird even the most inexplicable event.

Many contemplatives describe ways of being open and listening to God at all times. The most famous is perhaps Brother Lawrence's precious book, *The Practice of the Presence of God*. Before doing his manual work in the monastery, he prayed:

> O my God, since Thou are with me, and I must now, in obedience to Thy commands, apply my mind to these outward things, I beseech Thee to grant me the grace to continue in Thy presence; and to this end do Thou prosper me with Thy assistance, receive all my works, and possess all my affections.[8]

Being present to God in our lives means valuing each moment of our lives. Reality is not only in the future or in the past. We serve God in the present, we listen to God now. When God calls us, God does not want us to respond on some vague unspecified day in the future. God calls us today, here, and now.

The purpose of times of prayer and withdrawal, then, is to teach us how to be aware of God at all times. Gradually, ever so gradually, we learn that God addresses us in the present. Brother Lawrence worked in a monastery kitchen, "to which he had naturally a great aversion . . . ."[9] Even so, because of his mindfulness of God's presence, he could declare:

> The time of business . . . does not with me differ from the time of prayer; and in the noise and clatter of my kitchen, while several persons are at the same time calling for different things, I possess God in as great tranquillity as if I were upon my knees at the blessed sacrament."[10]

Our current ecological crises are in part related to our disconnectedness from God's presence. Nature is, in fact, one of the places where God's word comes to us. God created the world good and speaks to us through it. But we have chosen to see it as something to possess, control, manipulate, and even plunder. We do not treat it with the respect it deserves, lovingly cultivating it. Rather, we try to get all we can out of it, forgetting that God intends it to serve many creatures.

Our perceptions of what is around make all the difference in the world. As Elizabeth Barrett Browning wrote:

> Earth's crammed with heaven
> And every common bush afire with God;
> But only he who sees, takes off his shoes,
> The rest sit round it and pluck blueberries.

And thus Buechner is able to pray:

There is no ground anywhere that is not holy ground, for in the cool of the evening thou hast walked upon it and in the heat of the day thou hast died upon it, and at the coming of dawn thou hast returned and art always and everywhere returning to it and to us who walk upon it too, the holy ground, though heedless of its holiness.[11]

But nature is only one of the places where God addresses us. It "is the work of God. And yet God is not there; but within the individual . . . there is potentiality . . . which is awakened in inwardness . . . and then it becomes possible to see God everywhere."[12] The great thing is to be aware of God's presence everywhere. At all times—quiet and noisy, restful and active, and in all places—country or city, monastery or soup kitchen—God addresses us. "Holy, holy, holy is the Lord of hosts; the whole earth is full of his glory" (Isa. 6:3).

Nowhere are we separate from God, except by our own choice. No natural or even supernatural force has the power to cleave us from God's loving embrace, for "neither death, nor life, nor angels, nor principalities . . . will be able to separate us from the love of God in Christ Jesus our Lord" (Rom. 8:38-39).

TEN

Praying Always and Petitioning Prayer

Unceasing Prayer

We are called always to live in the awareness of God's presence. Tradition calls this awareness, "unceasing prayer." Paul mysteriously advised, "Rejoice always, pray constantly, give thanks in all circumstances; for this is the will of God in Christ Jesus for you" (1 Thess. 5:16-18). But that advice often perplexes us. A friend finds himself imprisoned for life. In our exchange of letters, we often discuss prayer. One day, he wrote:

> Did not Paul speak of unending prayer through all the day? I thought, at the first of my journey, that this guy had to be wrong because if I spent the whole day praying how could anyone get anything done. Now I spend more time listening, recognizing this is prayer, and speaking less, which is also prayer, and pray for larger parts of my day while tasks are completed.

Paul's advice about unceasing prayer does not necessarily mean focusing on God always and constantly, to the exclusion of everything and everyone around us. Rather, unceasing prayer means to focus on where we are and who we are with, knowing that God can address us through them. Prayer, then, does not take us out of life but is the consciousness of living in God's presence and God's time, "keeping company with God."

Quaker scholar Douglas V. Steere gives us a marvelous definition of prayer. "To pray is to pay attention to the deepest thing that we know."[1] Paying attention is not easy. Diversions and distractions abound. Yet our hearts need to recall and dwell on the deepest thing that we know.

And what is that? Simply that God loves us and desires intimate relationships with us, "for his steadfast love endures for ever" (Ps. 136). The Psalms give a good summary of unceasing prayer.

"For thy steadfast love is before my eyes,
  and I walk in faithfulness to thee" (Ps. 26:3).

By keeping God's steadfast love "before my eyes," by paying attention to the deepest thing we know, we are empowered to walk in faithfulness before God, to keep company with God. In a personal conversation, Henri Nouwen recommended that I become a mystic. "To be a mystic, I mean that God is the one who loves us deeply. And that's what you have to trust. Keep trusting, keep trusting, keep trusting."

Prayerfully repeating certain phrases helps me stay aware of "the deepest thing I know." The Orthodox have a tradition of the so-called "Jesus prayer." This is helpfully explored in a strangely wonderful book called *The Way of a Pilgrim*.[2] A simple Russian pilgrim wanted to know what it meant to "pray without ceasing." He went many places, read his Bible, heard numerous sermons, but no one could help him understand unceasing prayer.

Finally, a wise man instructed the Pilgrim to repeat one phrase constantly, the Jesus Prayer. "Lord Jesus Christ, have mercy on me."[3] This is derived from the humble prayer of the Publican, "God, be merciful to me a sinner!" (Luke 18:13). *The Way of a Pilgrim* recounts the Pilgrim's learnings and experiences in his practice of repetitively reciting the Jesus Prayer through his whole day and in all his life.

This prayer may seem odd to us. Those of us who are Anabaptists, with our suspicion of rituals, might look askance at such a practice. Jesus warned us that repetition is not effective in and of itself. "And in praying do not heap up empty phrases as the Gentiles do; for they think that they will be heard for their many words" (Matt. 6:7). The issue is how we use such a prayer. We do not pray the Jesus Prayer as a way of saving ourselves. That is to use prayer as means and technique and to regard it as magical.

> This repetition has nothing to do with magic. It is not meant to throw a spell on God or to force him into hearing us. On the contrary, a word or sentence repeated frequently can help us to concentrate, to move to the center, to create an inner stillness and thus listen to the voice of God.[4]

For various periods in my life, I have practiced the Jesus Prayer and found it helpful. It reminds me repeatedly, constantly, and everywhere of the deepest thing I know. It does not change God or God's attitude to me. But it reminds me of God's relationship to me and slowly changes me. There have been times when I was about to utter a harsh word and then heard the Jesus Prayer from within. "Lord Jesus Christ, have mercy on me." Suddenly I was unable to sin with my mouth.

This prayer can be an active reminder of God's presence and God's demand. I sadly confess that at times its reminder is too much for me. I don't want to hear or know. There were times I deliberately stopped praying the prayer, so I could sin. For what is sin, but rejecting the presence of God?

There is nothing magical about this formula. Many short, simple phrases can be helpful. "The Lord loves me," or "I am held by God" are other alternatives.

> The way of simple prayer, when we are faithful to it and practice it at regular times, slowly leads us to an experience of rest and opens us to God's active presence. Moreover, we can take this prayer with us into a very busy day. When, for instance, we have spent twenty minutes in the early morning sitting in the presence of God with the words "The Lord is my Shepherd" they may slowly build a little nest for themselves in our heart and stay there for the rest of our busy day.[5]

There are other ways of looking at this suggestion. Some Christians memorize Scriptures or meditate on Bible verses at the beginning of the day. Often, they choose to carry that Scripture with them all day, repeating it and mulling it over, paying attention to the deepest thing they know. They are amazed at how such a verse focuses and frames the day in new and un-expected ways.

The best base for such a practice is regular and disciplined times of silence. There, we begin to concentrate on our repeated phrase. It aids us in dealing with the distractions that sometimes trouble us during prayer. One author likes the phrase "I belong to God" and points out that it can help us turn even our rambling thoughts into prayer!

> And as you say "I belong to God," you will realize "so do all these things I've been thinking." "I wonder how the children are?" They belong to God. "Will I pass the exam?" That worry belongs to God. "Will I make it through this time of suffering?" I belong to God even when depressed or in pain. "Wasn't that a terrific party last night?" My joy also belongs to God. In some such way the thoughts that come to mind can become part of prayer rather than a disturbance to prayer.[6]

Audacity to Believe, by Sheila Cassidy, is one of the most impressive testimonies I have ever read. In it, I learned another practical way to pay attention to the deepest thing we know. Cassidy, a British M.D., moved to Chile to practice medicine. There, she was moved by the great poverty around her to minister and address issues of injustice. As well, she became a Christian.

Because of her faith, Cassidy ended up treating an enemy of the state and thereby made herself such an enemy. For her act of mercy, she was arrested, tortured horribly by electrical shock, and imprisoned in appalling circumstances.

In prison, Cassidy prayed. Resting on a lower bunk in her cell, she looked at the metallic mesh that held up the upper mattress. In its intersections and weavings, she saw a cross.

> I had long ago learned to look for the sign of the cross in doors and windows and all things square, for it reminded me of Christ and helped me to focus my attention on him and pray in unlikely places such as the bus or the hospital. . . . As I lay now and looked at the cross above my head I longed to leave some Christian sign upon this terrible place and wondered how I could mark for others the cross that I could see so clearly in the metal above me.[7]

She wound a strip of black wool around the cross that she could see.

Cassidy miraculously experienced God's solace and comfort in her imprisonment. "Incredibly, in the midst of fear and loneliness I was filled with joy, for I knew . . . God was with me, and that nothing that they could do to me could change that."[8] Cassidy was paying attention to the deepest thing she knew.

God is not only Lord over our lives when we withdraw into prayer closets. Rather, God is Lord everywhere and always. Being aware of that reality is to pray unceasingly. Prayer is not part-time. The purpose of occasional times of intense prayer is to remind us that all of our lives hang on God and rest in God. By our special-focus prayers, the whole of our lives become focused on God's presence with us.

Prayers of Petition

Many spiritual disciplines (silence, solitude, worship, fasting) easily fit into the paradigms that we have explored—openness and emptiness, listening to God in life, being present and available. Yet there is one discipline that often creates confusion and may not seem to fit these metaphors: prayer of petition. It needs to be considered as a possible exception to what we have been saying. It has, of course, a long and authoritative tradition and is amply authorized by the Scriptures.

There are considerable hazards and problems with many of the understandings and practices of prayers of petition. One need not watch trite and blasphemous Christian television to know about these abuses. The now-discredited Tammy Faye Bakker of the PTL Club claimed that God loaded her down with diamonds—each worth thousands of dollars—because God wants to give you "the desires of your heart" and "I like jewelry, it's fun for me."

Examples abound of such misunderstandings about prayer. Recently I picked up a hitchhiker in the middle of the morning. We chatted and he asked about my work. When I mentioned that I am a pastor, he responded, "Praise the Lord! Are you born again?"

This seemed somehow disrespectful. But I kept my resentment to myself. I observed that it was a strange time for a work shift to start. He did not get up early enough for the company bus, so for a week he hitchhiked to work, arriving, anywhere from one to three hours late.

"I just pray that the Lord will give my bosses understanding hearts," he said. *Better to invest in an alarm clock and pray for help in waking on time,* thought I.

Prayer is primarily relinquishing to God. It is a process of openness, where one permits God to intervene and convert us. Thus it should not be seen as merely asking God to make things different. Prayer is not effective in a mechanistic sense—do the right thing and God will automatically do what you want. God is personal, not a machine. "We want something from him, not him at all. Is that a relationship?"[9] No!

Nevertheless, abuses do not invalidate prayers of petition. On the contrary, petitionary prayer is a manifestation of our emptiness before and dependence on God. Jesus encouraged us to give our petitions to God. Petition need not be a misuse that invalidates all prayer or harms the rest of our prayer life.

> Far from ruining the purity of ... prayer, petition guards and preserves that purity. . . . Since [a person of prayer] depends directly on God for everything material and spiritual, he has to ask for everything. His prayer is an expression of his poverty.[10]

Thus petitioning God is one aspect of being open to God. Specific requests are acts and statements of faith.

> Our numerous requests simply become the concrete way of saying that we trust in the fullness of God's goodness, which he wants to share with us. Whenever we pray with hope, we put our lives in the hands of God.[11]

Asking of God is not a get-rich-scheme. Rather, we pray to remain open to God's will and always reliant on God. Thus prayers of petition are also an integral part of faithful spirituality.

Ultimately, all prayer—even prayers of petition and intercession—seek to align us more deeply in the ways and purposes of God. In the Lord's Prayer, we say:

Thy kingdom come
Thy will be done,
On earth as it is in heaven (Matt. 6:10).

In his agony in the Garden of Gethsemane, Jesus dared to make his bold request and at the same time submitted himself to God's will. "Father, if thou art willing, remove this cup from me; nevertheless not my will, but thine, be done" (Luke 22:42). Such prayers can only be prayed as we are confident of God's providence.

All this is not to say that our prayers accomplish nothing. There is a paradox here. For God gives us power in prayer. Even so, this relinquished ability is God-given and always beyond our control. It is true that prayers are fruitful and effective. "The prayer of a righteous man has great power in its effects" (James 5:16b). But the fruit, "effects" if you will, are always beyond our prediction and manipulation.

In his novel, *Godric*, Buechner discusses the unpredictability of prayer. Godric the saint has apparently not accomplished much that was visible or impressive, except to pray.

> What's prayer? It's shooting shafts into the dark. What mark they strike, if any, who's to say? It's reaching for a hand you cannot touch. The silence is so fathomless that prayers like plummets vanish in the sea. You beg. You whimper. You load God down with empty praise. You tell him sins that he already knows full well. You seek to change his changeless will. Yet Godric prays the way he breathes, for else his heart would wither in his breast. Prayer is the wind that fills his sail. Else waves would dash him on the rocks, or he would drift with witless tides.[12]

In Amos 7, the prophet has visions of a locust plague and a heavenly fire that threaten to destroy Israel. But Amos does not merely resign himself to God's will. He intercedes on behalf of Israel. Two times God repented or relented. " 'It shall not be,' said the Lord" (Amos 7:3; cf. 7:6). God's will is decided, worked, and apparently even changed in conjunction with his servants' prayers.

Although Amos expends considerable energy denouncing the sin of Israel, he also feels free to plead with God on Israel's behalf. As a prophet, he is God's agent, but he does not always have to agree with God. Rather, he may even argue with God!

The prayer of God's servants can have marvelous effects. Walter Wink shows that Daniel's prayers actually gave God new options. Thus it is that

> Daniel's intercessions have made possible the intervention of God. Prayer changes us, but it also changes what is possible for God. Daniel's cry was heard . . . it opened an aperture for God to act. . . . It inaugurated war in heaven. It opened a way through the impenetrable spirituality of foreign hegemony in order to declare a new and real divine possibility.[13]

God actually calls us to be interceders with him on behalf of his kingdom. God needs us to do that.

Intercession, Nagging for God, and the Struggle for Justice

> And he told them a parable, to the effect that they ought always to pray and not lose heart. He said, "In a certain city there was a judge who neither feared God nor regarded man; and there was a widow in that city who kept coming to him and saying, 'Vindicate me against my adversary.' For a while he refused; but afterward he said to himself, 'Though I neither fear God nor regard man, yet because this widow bothers me, I will vindicate her, or she will wear me out by her continual coming.' " And the Lord said, "Hear what the unrighteous judge says. And will not God vindicate his elect, who cry to him day and night? Will he delay long over them? I tell you, he will vindicate them speedily. Nevertheless, when the Son of man comes, will he find faith on earth?" (Luke 18:1-8).

In chapter two, we saw that widows had special significance in the biblical understanding of justice. Legal provisions and guarantees were made for all economically vulnerable people such as widows, orphans, the handicapped, and foreigners (e.g., Exod. 22:21-24; Deut. 27:19). Isaiah, for one, condemns those who refuse justice to widows (10:2) and makes a typically biblical recommendation:

> learn to do good;
> seek justice,
> correct oppression,
> defend the fatherless,
> plead for the widow (Isa. 1:17).

God commits widows to the responsible care of the faithful community.

Ignoring a widow's cry for justice, then, is catastrophically wicked. Apathetic about Yahweh's priorities, the judge in the parable neither fears God nor respects humans. Despising God is the immoral equivalent of ignoring justice. Day after day, this evil judge obstinately disregards the widow's appeal.

Contrasted with the unmerciful judge is a noteworthy liberator. A woman in a sexist, patriarchal society, her widowhood makes her a vulnerable among vulnerables. When she does not receive her due, she returns daily, imploring, demanding, and begging. She is only a woman, just a widow, merely a poor victim.

With neither privilege nor status, she nevertheless wins a victory. Her steadfastness has a tremendous power that is often underestimated by those enamored with political manipulation and coercion. The judge complains about her tenaciousness—"she will wear me out by her continual coming."

Clarence Jordan translates the woman's action as nagging. That word, so often used against women, is rightly suspected by feminists. Nagging, though, is often the only tool that powerless people have. Rather than being silenced by familiar accusations ("Stop nagging me!"), the widow persists. Jesus commends her controversial example, a nag par excellence.[14]

Surprisingly, Luke noted from the start that this parable is about prayer. Some conclude from this that we ought to pray long and hard, closeting ourselves for hours and haranguing God with long diatribes. But this interpretation misses the point, as a distorted notion of prayer skews the story. In fact, without the first verse, many would never guess that the parable is about prayer. Some commentators even believe the first verse is wrong! That says more about their misunderstanding of prayer than it does about the parable.

In fact, the woman's actions are prayer. To work for justice is prayer. To agitate, protest, and persist for the sake of liberation is prayer. Prayer is other things as well—but it cannot be separated from these concerns and such activities. To make a nuisance of oneself, nagging for God's justice and righteousness, is to do

God's work and to be in prayer. When we pray, God works through us. Thus Jesus' final question is crucial to God's compassionate outreach: when the Son comes, will faith be found on earth?

Some believe that justice should be blind, objective, neutral, and passion-free. Abraham Heschel observes that our human

> sense of injustice is a poor analogy to God's sense of injustice. The exploitation of the poor is to us a misdemeanor; to God it is a disaster. Our reaction is disapproval; God's reaction is something no language can convey.[15]

God is grief-stricken when no one intervenes against oppression.

> The Lord saw it, and it displeased him
> that there was no justice.
> He saw that there was no man,
> and wondered that there was no one to intervene (Isa. 59:15b-16a).

God counts on us for such work.

> In a sense, the calling of the prophet may be described as that of an advocate or champion, speaking for those who are too weak to plead their own cause. Indeed the major activity of the prophets was interference, remonstrating about wrongs inflicted on other people, meddling in affairs which were seemingly neither their concern nor their responsibility.[16]

God is heartened by people like the widow who nags her way toward God's kingdom. Our history is full of such liberating examples. Harriet Tubman, Sojourner Truth, and Fannie Lou Hamer were black women who all experienced significant institutional oppression (two were slaves and one a sharecropper). They faithfully advanced God's cause.

More recently, we can look to the relatives of the "disappeared" in Latin America. During Argentina's last military junta, grieving mothers and widows of the disappeared gathered together regularly in public to protest and demand information about their loved ones. Their nagging persistence had a high price. Some disappeared themselves. But the movement was not deterred. Some were taken to prisons and heard the anguished screams of the tortured. They grew more resolved. Others received the ears of loved ones as bloody threats.

It did not work. The widows persisted, silently pleading and grieving for those they loved. By now they have a limited victory. The new government has tried some officials responsible for atrocities.

In Guatemala, mothers and widows of the disappeared form the only open human rights organization. All others are either destroyed or driven underground. They risk much for their courage. For them, Jesus' promise is especially relevant. "And will not God vindicate his elect. . .? I tell you, he will vindicate them speedily."

The parable makes no promise about what we will accomplish. The success is God's and God's alone. We cannot manipulate God into acting. God does not vindicate because we are tenacious. We persist in the confidence that God hears us and that God will ultimately succeed. God works for justice and we know that is central to God's character. We are steadfast because of our faith in who God is and our steadfastness is intimately bound up with faithful spirituality.

Holy Interference

Theilisma René greatly inspired me in my understanding of prayerful lives. In spite of threats, arrests, dangerous political situations, and bleak prospects for his country Haiti, he perseveres in working toward God's reign.

René, a Roman Catholic lay person, is an encourager, motivator, and organizer in a parish program in the area surrounding Mombin Crochu, a poor mountain village in northeastern Haiti. The program helps organize base communities throughout the mountains. Like an early apostle, René often walks for miles up and down steep, rocky paths to attend weekly meetings of the communities.

This movement is based on the *ti legliz* (Creole for "little church"). Small groups of fifteen to thirty people gather weekly to pray, sing, study the Bible, educate themselves, and deal with personal, pastoral, practical, and political problems.

Each *ti legliz* works differently and establishes its own sense of purpose. But they all maintain close contact with other *ti leglizes*. A delegate system encourages mutual accountability and enables cooperation on major projects. The movement involves at least sixteen hundred peasants and fostered unparalleled cooperation between Protestants and Roman Catholics.

The movement models itself after the early church in Acts 4. Group members pool money and resources so they can care for members' needs. Sometimes they invest together in a garden to increase their resources or jointly make major purchases—such as plows or oxen. In a society where impoverishment is normal and it is impossible to save money, the ti leglizes offer new and almost unimaginable options. Each community is voluntary. But their successes make them attractive and inspire others to be more faithful or even to join. It's what Clarence Jordan considered evangelism by demonstration.

I met and spoke with René in 1986, the year that Jean Claude ("Baby Doc") Duvalier abandoned his dictatorship and fled Haiti. René first became involved in the church as a child through church plays, service as an altar boy, and the youth movement. He eventually became a teacher.

Indebted to the nuns for an education that as an orphan he could not afford, René committed his life to serving God through the church. In addition to raising seven children with his wife, Dye Lajis (her name means "God is just"), he was involved in many church activities. When I spoke with him, he was president of the parish advisory committee, a member of its youth committee, a leader in the national youth movement, and a participant in the diocesan advisory committee.

René also works with the Committee on Justice and Peace, a national organization which monitors human-rights violations, a subject that he knows firsthand. In 1981, he was tagged as an agitator because of his congregational work. He was arrested and jailed. After a day without food or water, he was taken to Vallieres, a four-hour walk through the mountains.

René believes his life was spared because he defended himself with remembered portions of Duvalier's rhetoric. With all the boldness of the widow before the unjust judge, he quoted

Duvalier speeches that encouraged social and economic development. Then he told his captors, "That's the line I'm working on."

Not content to absolve himself, he asked the district commander to bring the prefect, mayor, and deputy. They were the real criminals, he said. They stole land, imprisoned people for no reason, and didn't contribute to the zone's development. He stood ready to accuse them before Duvalier himself, whose speeches they disobeyed.

René was being not just prophetic, but canny as well. Vallieres was isolated and did not receive its share of government and funding. So the locals agreed with him and released him. They even offered him a position in the local government. He declined.

Despite the dangers, René continued to take great risks because of his faith. In 1985, he was the only person in his village to vote against Duvalier. At two polling stations he noted that the soldiers controlling the voting handed out only yes ballots. Wanting to know if people really had a choice, he asked for and received a "no" ballot at a third station.

A soldier then pointed a gun at him asked, "Does this mean you are against our President-for-Life?" René replied that he did not oppose any president but only the words "for life." He was taken, with a gun held to his neck, to another polling station to await the sergeant. But he was later released without further harassment.

René strives tirelessly for his vision, a vision as big as God's reign and looks forward to everyone having faith in God. He knows that faith precludes violence and oppression. So he works for the day when everyone in Haiti can claim civil and political rights without intimidation, have good education, and have access to proper health care.

Yet his hopes are rooted in a faith nurtured by other believers. Because of his magnificent vision, I was startled when he told me that he had no hope for beneficial political changes in the near future. (At this writing, some years later, I know that he was unfortunately correct). Too many groups strive for power in Haiti, wanting to impose their own selfish "solutions." Thus

René is committed to the long process of converting and empowering the Haitian people from the ground up.

For me, Mombin Crochu was impressive evidence of the church's potential to create new options. Here, as everywhere in Haiti, people suffered vast corruption and injustice. But through many upheavals in the country, Mombin Crochu is one of the least violent areas. Nevertheless, like the people of Israel, says René, Haitians have only crossed the Red Sea and are still facing the wilderness. I remain greatly impressed by the resolute witness of people who face down the unjust judges of the world in the name of God's kingdom on earth as in heaven. Their example has too little influenced our understanding and practice of prayer.

ELEVEN

Toward a Spirituality for Kingdom Workers

Where Have All the Flower Children Gone?

It is now over two decades later, but myths about the '60s continue to grow and abound. Some believe that the younger generation of that time almost changed the world.

But what happened after that? Where is the fervor and passion of those turbulent years? What happened to the activism and commitment during those troubled times? Instead of creating a new society, many of the former hippies and yippies have now joined the very "Establishment" they formerly despised, perpetuating the values they once opposed.

The lesson is instructive. For many—indeed most—of the issues raised by that angry generation are still important and relevant: wealth and poverty, race, the environment, war and peace. Their protests were not meaningless. Rather, the problem was that they were not sufficiently rooted in an alternative reality. Too much of their energy was merely generated by normal youthful anger and self-concern.

The draft was a major reason some became countercultural. With the threat of the draft removed, many were no longer passionate about the '60s agenda. Their commitment to an alternative lifestyle and society was often rooted only in their own selfish agenda.

Recall Jesus' words, "Other seeds fell on rocky ground, where

144

they had not much soil, and immediately they sprang up, since they had no depth of soil, but when the sun rose they were scorched; and since they had no root they withered away" (Matt. 13:5-6).

There are those, of course, whose radical witness extended and lasted through and beyond the sixties: Dan and Phil Berrigan, Liz McAlister, Jim Douglass, James Forest, Dorothy Day, Cesar Chavez. All had one thing in common—a Christian faith deeply nourished in prayer.

As followers of Jesus, we are emissaries of his kingdom. We are called to live and do the reality of God's kingdom here and now. We represent and reflect God's reality, which is opposed to the ways of the world. Paul instructed us, "Do not be conformed to this world . . ." (Rom. 12:2a). But this is a hard and overwhelming task. It cannot be done solely through our own resources.

We face many dangers. We may be overcome by all that opposes us. We may wither under the opposition. Or we may try to do too much. In busyness, we might lose sight of our true purpose. Paul reminds us that the nonconformity is connected to inner renewal and change: "Be transformed by the renewal of your mind, that you may prove what is the will of God, what is good and acceptable and perfect" (Rom. 12:2b).

We need to be prayerful people, if we are going to do God's work. "The more numerous our commitments, the more diverse our work, the more time-consuming our participation, then the more we should stop and contemplate the only source of all action, Jesus Christ."[1]

Jesus counseled that godly action can only be done in him. "I am the vine, you are the branches. He who abides in me, and I in him, he it is that bears much fruit, for apart from me you can do nothing" (John 15:5).

Holy Uselessness

In our Western passion for productivity, we exalt means and doing over ends and being. Not surprisingly, such false distinctions are rejected by many who advise us in matters of spirituality. We do not deal here only with an either-or issue. Often means and ends are inseparable.

We have already seen how some try to misuse prayer or God for their own ends. Prayer is actually radical protest against all reliance on human effectiveness; "prayer in the Scriptures is . . . a renunciation of human means."[2]

Proponents of nonviolence assert that the end does not justify the means as they are the same thing. Prayer and nonviolence are both rooted in the conviction that our reliance must be primarily in God. "The chief difference between nonviolence and violence is that the latter depends entirely on its own calculations. The former depends entirely on God and on His word."[3]

Alas, in our means-oriented society doing is exalted over being. Productivity determines worth. Thus all who are not productive are worthless. This is reflected in the devaluation of such groups that do not produce according to our standards, including minorities, unemployed, poor, elderly, handicapped, and even fetuses and embryos. Things and means become more valuable than people. Yet we recall from our previous Bible study that those groups most despised in the world are of a special priority to God.

> When we start being too impressed by the results of our work, we slowly come to the erroneous conviction that life is one large scoreboard where someone is listing the points to measure our worth. And before we are fully aware of it, we have sold our soul to the many grade-givers. That means we are not only in the world, but also of the world. Then we become what the world makes us.[4]

Our worth is not rooted in what we have accomplished or done, but in our value as beings in God's image who are saved by God's gracious redemption. In other words, our worth is related to the old theological issue of grace and works. Our works do not make us valuable. We are worthwhile because of what God has done for us. Much in this world may not be deemed useful or productive but is nevertheless valuable because of God and God's priorities.

Henri Nouwen's spiritual journey led him from working with the "best and brightest" in the Ivy League spheres of Yale and Harvard to a "hidden" and quiet life in a l'Arche community in

Canada. L'Arche is an international network of communities where mentally handicapped persons and their assistants seek to live together according to the gospel.

Nouwen found that in the busy world of academia and ambition, many people made great demands on him. In an interview during October 1988, he told me that mentally handicapped people taught him about God's kind of love. "I also realized that handicapped people didn't love or care for me because I write books or take trips. They don't know that. If they express love, it comes from God." This community, with a perspective so radically different than the world's, has changed Nouwen's priorities.

> I still get invitations to speak all over the world, but I have to say no. My community says it's more important to stay here instead of flying all over. It's more important to spend an evening with someone who can't speak or do anything, than speak to thousands of people.

The spiritual experience of being part of l'Arche has reoriented Nouwen's whole life.

> These broken, wounded and completely unpretentious people forced me to let go of my relevant self—the self that can do things, show things, prove things, build things—and forced me to reclaim that unadorned self in which I am completely vulnerable, open to receive and give love regardless of any accomplishments.

Worth need not be tied to effectiveness or usefulness. We often assign greatest worth to things that are in fact effectively useless.

> A carpenter and his apprentice were walking together through a large forest. And when they came across a tall, huge, gnarled, old, beautiful oak tree, the carpenter asked his apprentice: "Do you know why this tree is so tall, so huge, so gnarled, so old and beautiful?" The apprentice looked at his master and said:
> "No . . . why?"
> "Well," the carpenter said, "because it is useless. If it had been useful it would have been cut long ago and made into tables and chairs, but because it is useless it could grow so tall and so beautiful that you can sit in its shade and relax."[5]

Earlier we saw that the God of the Bible, God incarnate, is the God of the useless. Thus we have an important reason to value what the world does not. "God chose what is foolish in the world to shame the wise, God chose what is weak in the world to shame the strong . . ." (1 Cor. 1:27-29).

Thus, not surprisingly, "there is more help and healing in silence than in all the 'useful things.' "[6] We follow a God who failed, a crucified messiah, a fool. Yet it is our conviction that the ineffective actions of that simpleton are more important than any other event in history. Truman considered the atomic bombing of Hiroshima to be "the greatest thing in history." But our view of history is much different. "It is pure materialism to regard only the audible facts of history as important."[7]

Prayer is silent, useless, and nonproductive according to worldly values. It is not humanly effective.

> Prayer is ridiculed because its effectiveness is entirely unpredictable, and statistical techniques are able to show that the percentage of "answers" to prayer corresponds exactly to the percentage of success which would have been the case had events been allowed to take their own course, and without prayer.[8]

Some argue that prayer is effective because the "prayer of a righteous man has great power in its effects" (James 5:16b). The Bible does promise that prayer brings results. Still we do not control prayer. The very meaning of prayer—and of all faithful spiritual disciplines—is one of uselessness as the world measures utility.

> Prayer is not a way of being busy with God instead of with people. In fact, it unmasks the illusion of busyness, usefulness, and indispensability. It is a way of being empty and useless in the presence of God and so of proclaiming our basic belief that all is grace and nothing is simply the result of hard work.[9]

In our society, faithful prayer is both protest and resistance to what others value most highly.

This "holy uselessness" gives us a freedom we do not find in the world. We do not have to be successful to be worthwhile in God's eyes. Rather, Jesus is our model. Our hope comes from his crucifixion and resurrection, not from a worldly and mechanistic notion of effectiveness.

> The triumph of the right is assured not by the might that comes to the aid of the right . . . the triumph of the right, although it is assured, is sure because of the power of the resurrection and not because of any calculation of causes and effects, nor because of the inherently greater strength of the good guys. The relationship between the obedience of God's people and the triumph of God's cause is not a relationship of cause and effect but one of cross and resurrection.[10]

This hope is deepened in prayer because we grow to depend and rely upon God, listening to him. Direct effects are not what we live for. We cannot and dare not rely merely on being useful.

> Do not depend on the hope of results. When you are doing the sort of work you have taken on . . . you have to face the fact that your work will be apparently worthless and even achieve no result at all, if not perhaps results opposite to what you expect. As you get used to this idea, you start more and more to concentrate not on the results but on the value, the rightness, the truth of the work itself.[11]

"For the foolishness of God is wiser than men, and the weakness of God is stronger than men" (1 Cor. 1:25). As Christ's fools, we have more in common with clowns than with technocrats. It is a ministry, a comic relief, a grace, that there are a few who are not useful . . . and do not even try to be. "Amidst so many 'useful' people we should keep reminding ourselves of our basic uselessness and so bring a smile and a little humor to all we do."[12]

Being freed to fail, we can rely on the goodness and providence of God even as we serve God. "All the good that you do will come not from you but from the fact that you have allowed yourself, in the obedience of faith, to be used by God's love."[13]

The Feast of Fools

Christian spirituality changes all our perspectives. This is seen clearly in our celebration of the Lord's Supper. One reason the Romans persecuted the early church was because of popular misunderstandings about communion. They even suspected Christians of committing cannibalism! Its implications are no less radical today.

Even now, some consider the vivid imagery of body and blood inappropriately grim for a celebration. Every time we celebrate the Lord's Supper, we recall the horrible events of Holy Week. We remember what happened to Jesus on that grievous Friday, so-called Good—the day our hope was extinguished. The feast does not end with despair, of course. It always points us beyond to the hope that is ours, the resurrection triumph of Easter Sunday.

As we celebrate communion, our minds turn to harrowing realities within the wider knowledge of Christ's resurrection. With that crucial assurance, we are able to face the hard questions that beset everyone. "For as often as you eat this bread and drink the cup, you proclaim the Lord's death until he comes" (1 Cor. 11:26). In our faith, we are freed to explore, endure, and accept realities that others prefer to avoid.

The disturbing imagery of the broken, bleeding, battered body are the stuff of despair. Jesus cried out, "My God, my God, why hast thou forsaken me?" (Mark 15:33). And such lamentations remain with us today. Canadian singer Bruce Cockburn sings:

> So how come history takes such a long, long time
> When you're waiting for a miracle?[14]

Communion points us to the place where our deepest and most bitter questions dwell. It frees us to engage them. We do not avoid the questions but pass through them, as the Israelites passed through the Red Sea, to the place where God heals and saves us. Henri Nouwen writes:

> The Good News of the Gospel is that the death of Christ was the gateway to new life. I think that the story of Christ's death can only be told as a story of hope by those whose faith is deeply anchored in his resurrection. Just as sin can only be truly known to us in the light of forgiving grace, so death can only be faced squarely in the light of the new life to which it leads. This is important to realize when we want to see not only the death but also the resurrection of Christ as

part of the historical reality in which we live. Maybe we have to say that only in the context of the new life that we see being born out of human agonies are we able to face these very agonies.[15]

Communion celebrations that particularly touch and tear me take place at a Catholic Worker shelter in Detroit's inner city. They are earthy, rambunctious and, yes, holy events. A wide variety of people crowd together into a huge, peeling house just two blocks from Tiger Stadium and several blocks from the area where the 1967 riots occurred. Sitting on and around battered old furniture, we pack ourselves into two faded rooms that are used as emergency bedrooms at night.

The service is directly relevant to life, ministry, and work in Detroit and the wider world. There, one daily sees the world's and our own brokenness with new and startling clarity. That communion service makes the urgency of God's good news especially clear. There, the gospel is not esoteric or theoretical; it is essential and indispensable. As I hear the gospel in that troubled context, conversion works and reworks in my heart.

The Lord's Supper—like worshiping in that Detroit shelter—does not move our attention away from pain and evil. In fact, it focuses us on the gruesome suffering of Jesus' death on the cross. Rather than turning us from the pain, confusion, and doubt of injustice, it confronts us with our own doubt and despair. It highlights the apparent senselessness of suffering.

For God does not work in ways that we understand, let alone appreciate.

> For my thoughts are not your thoughts,
> neither are your ways my ways, says the Lord.
> For as the heavens are higher than the earth,
> so are my ways higher than your ways
> and my thoughts than your thoughts (Isa. 55:8-9).

We want obedience to God to be connected with success in life. "Okay, God, we have been faithful to you long enough, now you owe us happiness, wealth, health, and honor." Unfortunately a large part of the church caters to this mentality, often with tragic results.

The flip side of that idea is the unhappy and mistaken notion that suffering is always God's punishment for our sins. Some time ago, an acquaintance of mine was raped. She was always taught that when you are faithful God guards you. But here, apparently, God lifted the umbrella of protection from her. She wondered if the rape was her fault. She must have sinned or God would have spared her.

But God does not work that way with us—or even with God! In fact, God deliberately enters into suffering—even though God does not deserve it. Likewise God also allows us to encounter tribulation and evil precisely because of our faithfulness. We are not insulated from all risk, danger, and pain.

Good friends of mine worked overseas with Mennonite Central Committee for three years. He left a secure, upwardly mobile, well-paying job in Canada. While remaining in the corporation, he was guaranteed promotions with a steady increase in benefits and salary for as long as he chose to stay. But God called him elsewhere. So they left security and comfort to live and work among the poor. God's will was more important than calculations about their future.

When the couple's assignment was completed, they returned to Canada. Since going abroad, they had grown as a family. Leaving childless, they returned with two children. Then began many long, hard months of waiting, worrying, and sweating. The security they left behind three years before was not easy to recover. Now, because of the added responsibility of children, that stability was urgent.

For a long while, he did not find any work. He experienced the usual anxiety and discouragement unemployment brings. He blamed himself. When he finally did find work, the job was neither rewarding nor fulfilling. It did not demand his best gifts and abilities. The wages paid were not enough to support a family of four.

The family endured much in the long months after they returned to Canada. I remember wondering what God was up to. Surely they had been faithful in a big way and surely they deserved God's special care.

But God does not necessarily work that way. Jesus Christ was always faithful and obedient to God. By our calculations, such a life deserves gracious rewards. But Jesus was not successful in life. He was a miserable failure, an embarrassment to family and friends. His success came not in life, but in enduring suffering and death.

There he was, in spite of all his powerful claims and deeds, weak and unprotected, defeated and hanging on a cross. People ridiculed him. He was arrayed in a bloody purple robe and a crown of thorns. Pilate hung a mocking sign over his head—the King of the Jews. Some king! Matthew tells us that passersby and witnesses derided, reviled, and mocked him (Matt. 27:39-44).

Jesus was ridiculed for looking like a fool. Even his closest friends were ashamed. He was betrayed for money by one of his own disciples. The others abandoned him. Jesus looked absurd. His enemies gloated over his shame and his friends cowered. Jesus, king of the buffoons.

Now any institution or religion with public relations savvy would cover up such facts about its founder. This just won't sell. This is not the way to win followers and influence people. But instead the gospels clearly and forthrightly spell out Jesus' folly. Even Paul, that exemplary church planter and evangelist, celebrates the embarrassment of Jesus' foolishness. "For the word of the cross is folly to those who are perishing, but to us who are being saved it is the power of God . . . (1 Cor. 1:18). This is a strange and unlikely church growth strategy.

In medieval times, there was a popular annual holiday called the Feast of Fools.

> On that colorful occasion . . . even ordinarily pious priests and serious townsfolk donned bawdy masks, sang outrageous ditties, and generally kept the whole world awake with revelry and satire. Minor clerics painted their faces, strutted about in the robes of their superiors, and mocked the stately rituals of Church and court. Sometimes a lord of misrule, a mock king or a boy bishop was elected to preside over the events. . . . During the Feast of Fools, no custom or convention was immune from ridicule and even the highest personages of the realm could expect to be lampooned.[16]

In Victor Hugo's novel, *Notre Dame of Paris*, the infamous hunchback Quasimodo was crowned as "fools' pope" during the Feast of Fools. During the Feast of Fools, the vulnerabilities and weaknesses of power and status were displayed and scorned. The Feast showed that a culture "could imagine, at least once in a while, a wholly different kind of world—one where the last was first, accepted values were inverted, fools became kings and choirboys were prelates."[17] For one brief day every year, the norms were upset and overturned; an upside-down kingdom was celebrated and the unexpected happened.

The Lord's Supper is a feast of fools, a time when we celebrate and proclaim the reversal of the world's values. We remember how our great leader served and washed feet. We are mindful that Jesus' greatest victory was won in death. We celebrate Jesus, King of kings and Fool of fools.

Good Friday is a feast of fools. What looks like the final defeat becomes the greatest victory. Because of Easter Sunday, the Shameful Friday becomes Good Friday. But we do not get to that Easter Sunday without first passing through that horrible Friday.

We want God to come in power to set everything right. But instead God comes in weakness and suffering to die. That is how God turns evil into good. That is not the way the world likes to work. But God's ways are above our ways. God's foolishness and weakness are mightier than our wisdom and strength.

During communion at the Detroit shelter, one can experience this reversal of the world's values in surprising and startling ways. A needy neighborhood friend was notorious for his bizarre non sequiturs, hardly the kind of person we would select (let alone ordain) to preach. Once he piped up during the passing of the cup, "They don't serve cocktails in the Kremlin." I did not even try to understand what he meant. Yet he was on to something. Surely, neither Moscow nor Washington nor Ottawa offer—or secure—God's communion. We must look elsewhere.

God could come in power and might to conquer evil and injustice. But who could escape such a judgment? We easily forget what we have done to and against God. But God invites us to the table of reconciliation, the Feast of Fools, anyway. Cockburn sings:

At the feast of fools
outlaws can all come home.[18]

In God's eyes, we were all outlaws and enemies. But God changed that. The Lord's table is a feast open to all who will absurdly follow Jesus the fool. Once we were criminals, but we are felons no longer. God reaches out to us in compassion and mercy, transforming us into heirs of the divine reign.

Thus we partake of communion together, in thankful remembrance of what God did for us, in gratitude for what God does for us, and in joyful anticipation of what God promises to all people. The meal is an oath of allegiance to the Reign of God. Eating Jesus' bread means committing ourselves to Jesus and drinking his cup means binding ourselves to Jesus and his foolish ways. It means giving up our lives in return as a thankful offering of ourselves to God.

This we do even to the point of looking nonsensical for Jesus' sake, even if it means dying for him. "We are fools for Christ's sake . . ." (1 Cor. 4:10a). Communion is a Feast of Fools.

Who in their right mind would choose to follow a king who washes dirty feet and then gets his body broken, punctured, bloody, and torn? What sane person would listen to the inane ways of Jesus? Who would turn their cheek in the face of violence? Who would wish to be meek? Who would choose to serve? Who would desire to be poor in spirit?

When invited to the Feast of Fools, we are faced with precisely those absurd choices. God enables us to choose the life and example of Christ, with all its costs and risks. No matter what we have done or who we have been, crazy Jesus keeps reaching out to us.

> I spread out my hands all the day
> to a rebellious people,
> who walk in a way that is not good,
> following their own devices (Isa. 65:2).

The Lord's meal is a chance to celebrate the love that God poured out, like wine into a cup—a life that God's own child poured out in love for our sake, a love that calls us to similar foolish sacrifice.

People prefer to avoid suffering. But that is not Christ's way. With him, we do not ignore or escape what others endure. In fact, Christ shows us that we too must enter into the pain and hurt of those around us. Only then do we move toward the reign of God. Only then do we live in the confidence of the resurrection. Where is hope? Where is joy? Where is the miracle we await? Where is God's reign? Again Cockburn sings.

> So I'm walking this prison camp world
> I long for a glimpse of
> the new world unfurled
> The chrysalis cracking and moisten
> wings uncurl
> Like in the vision John saw
> the vision John saw.[19]

The glimpse and the vision do not come through disregarding the brokenness around and within us. John had his visions as a prisoner on the island of Patmos.

Christ's meal points to a hope that is neither out of this world nor otherworldly. As we break bread and drink wine, we recall and celebrate Christ's shattered body and shed blood. Christian hope moves through and beyond suffering and death. Thus in many communion liturgies, believers proclaim together, "Christ has died! Christ has risen! Christ will come again!"

Many want to claim the benefits of the resurrection without following Jesus' suffering in this life. But as communion people we are enabled to live in the comfort and assurance of the resurrection, and thus are empowered to face the suffering and injustice all around. Our confidence in the resurrection gives us this capacity. So every Lord's Supper is a joyful and solemn feast for us fools who are waiting for a miracle.

TWELVE

The Greatest Spiritual Fruit

Compassion

[Compassion] is hard work; it is crying out with those in pain; it is tending the wounds of the poor and caring for their lives; it is defending the weak and indignantly accusing those who violate their humanity; it is joining with the oppressed in the struggle for justice; it is pleading for help, with all possible means, from any person who has ears to hear and eyes to see.[1]

Compassion is a central concern and priority for us. It is so integral to spirituality that without it our spiritual disciplines are invalid.

We encounter the unity of compassion and spirituality over and again. True prayer does not cut us off from compassion and people. "Praying can never be antisocial or asocial. Whenever you pray and leave out your fellow . . . your prayer is no longer real prayer."[2] Union with God is not possible if we are not somehow being drawn into deeper relationships with people as well.

Thus hell means not only separation from God but isolation from people. "Hell is where no one has anything in common with anybody else except the fact that they all hate one another and themselves."[3] Jean-Paul Sartre's play, *No Exit*, describes a room where three people are locked in with one another but can find no commonality, no community, no mutuality.

Spirituality and compassion are not separate but indivisible.

Spiritual disciplines are invalid if practiced in the context of injustice, as both Jesus and the prophets taught. Spiritual life is biblical only if the practitioner is compassionate or growing in compassion.

To love well we need to be integrally related to God. Thus time with God leads and reorients us to compassionate love. In prayer we grow in love, because in prayer we are open to the converting action of our loving God. If we want to grow in compassion we will spend time in prayer. Henri Nouwen spoke to me of the need to be in close touch with God's "first love."

> Those words "first love," are important to me. God loves us with a first love. John says, "Love one another, because I first loved you." The love of people is beautiful, but it's a reflection—a refraction, actually—of God's first love.

God's love, his compassion, are crucial. The Latin words from which *compassion* derives are *"pati* and *cum,* which together mean 'to suffer with.' Compassion asks us to share in brokenness, fear, confusion, and anguish."[4] Compassion is more than feeling sorry for another; it involves identifying with that other. Compassion means to recognize the deep and basic unity of all people. It is the awareness of the interconnectedness of all. Ultimately, our actions affect one other; we are not isolated from each other.

> Compassion teaches me that when my brother dies, I too die. Compassion teaches me that my brother and I are one. That if I love my brother, then my love benefits my own life as well, and if I hate my brother and seek to destroy him, I destroy myself also.[5]

Acknowledging our interdependence does not come easy in this society. We are more comfortable with competition. Compassion, the exact opposite of competition, is not our priority. "What we really desire is to . . . get ahead, to be first, to be different. We want . . . niches in life where we can remain a safe distance from others."[6]

Competition drives us apart, makes us rely only on ourselves, and causes us to worry about others harming us or at least doing better than we do. Compassion is the opposite of competition: it is interdependence. "In the temporal world a man may succeed in getting along without love . . . but in eternity he cannot dispense with love. . . ."[7] Compassion is divine and we must be divinely rooted to be compassionate. "Only God can be wholly compassionate because only he is not in competition with us."[8]

Compassion understood this way can be painful. If we are united to all, then we are united in pain and suffering as well. Remember that compassion means to "suffer with." Being aware of the pain that people suffer brings us pain too. Compassion means that we will suffer as long as our siblings suffer. Helpless before such pain, we are driven to prayer.

> A brother who was . . . put in prison after working among the poor in Argentina . . . writes: "What characterized our Christian life in prison was prayer, and more precisely, prayer of intercession. When you hear the despairing screams of your friends who are in the process of being tortured, and when you experience your total helplessness to do anything, you learn that to pray and to intercede is the only worthy human act that one is capable of doing.[9]

Compassionately praying for others is intercession, a particularly important form of prayer. By interceding, we rely on God because we know our inadequacy to be totally compassionate to and for them. Thus intercessory prayer is not just another spiritual discipline, it is a crucial discipline. Through it, God's priority of compassion is honored. Prayer, as well as being the base of compassion, roots us in compassion, and is an essential expression of compassion.

As we saw in the parable of the persistent widow, prayers of intercession drive us to witness and action on behalf of those who suffer. "In our solution-oriented society it is . . . important . . . to realize that wanting to alleviate pain without sharing it is like wanting to save a child from a burning house without . . . being hurt."[10]

But always, always, we must recall that our love, our work, our compassionate ministry is rooted in God himself. Nouwen learned this as well. He shared with me about a breakdown that he experienced.

> I was so broken, that finally God had a chance to speak to me. And
> he didn't say, "You should do something else or you better do some-
> thing else, go to the missions or work in Latin America or think
> about the poor." But, "Rest and let me love you."

In fact, God taught Nouwen the most important lesson about
love from the mentally handicapped who now live in community with him. God spoke to him, "Trust that you are loved. I sent
you these poor, poor people in this little community to tell you
that. It's not that you are for them. You are handicapped."

God's First-Strike Strategy

But it is not enough to learn love and compassion. Jesus challenges us to love even our enemies.

> God shows his love for us in that while we were yet sinners Christ
> died for us. Since, therefore, we are now justified by his blood, much
> more shall we be saved by him from the wrath of God. For if while
> we were enemies we were reconciled to God by the death of his
> Son, much more, now that we are reconciled, shall we be saved by
> his life" (Rom. 5:6-10).

God isn't the only one with enemies. I often think of one of
mine. Carefully I nurtured my grievances and grudges against
him. Content with our cold war, I did not talk to him for over a
year. Never mind that he too was a Christian or that I also
needed forgiveness. If we never spoke again, I wouldn't worry. It
seemed no problem for me to ignore Jesus' words when I
thought about this enemy.

In the end, however, my enemy defeated me—in a way that
was unexpected and unwelcome. Through no fault of mine, except my feeble attempts at faithfulness, I found myself prosecuted. I was, in fact, being persecuted. It was one of the hardest
times of my life. I felt so alone, needing friends and support.

At this troubled time, my enemy heard of my problems. He
called me up. I was surprised and taken aback to hear his voice
on the phone. He wished me well and offered his support. And
then he made good. He gave not only much-needed personal
support but even helped with legal costs.

I had not intended to be reconciled with my brother. But his surprise initiative disarmed me. Kierkegaard noted that the one who loves "has the last word."[11] My window of vulnerability was that I could not stop him from loving me. Like God, my brother knew that the best way to destroy an enemy is to befriend him. The significant reconciliation that resulted challenged me to continue the work of reconciliation with my other enemies.

Reconciliation is a mutual process that often begins unilaterally. Seldom do both enemies move simultaneously to cease hostility. Usually one gives in, reaches out, and makes peace possible. Such innovative efforts create new possibilities where before there was only hate. My new friend—and former enemy —ended a conflict and created peace with me. He brought healing to us both—and thereby furthered God's kingdom.

My friend imitated God, who repeatedly initiates reconciliation with us. History is filled with the gracious interventions of our loving God. Romans 5 reminds us of the unilateralism of Jesus' death. Christ died while we were yet sinners (enemies of the divine!), reconciling us to God.

Unilateral redemption at God's divine initiative was made with no demand of a peace proposal from humanity. No verification agreements were required. We were neither told to stop sinning first nor even given a treaty to sign. God just acted.

Jesus impossibly and unreasonably instructs us to "Love your enemies and pray for those who persecute you, so that you may be sons of your Father who is in heaven . . ." (Matt. 5:44-45a). It is by loving our enemies that our spiritual relationship as God's children is established. Elsewhere in the Sermon on the Mount, Jesus exhorts, "Blessed are the peacemakers, for they shall be called sons of God" (Matt. 5:9).

In mercy and love, we imitate God. "When you love your neighbor, then you are like unto God."[12] Following Jesus, who died for his enemies, involves us in the work of peace as agents of his reconciliation in an alienated and alienating world. "All this is from God, who through Christ reconciled us to himself and gave us the ministry of reconciliation . . ." (2 Cor. 5:18). And our love (or hate) for others reflects our relationship to God.

Imitating Jesus or following Jesus are vital concerns of spirituality. But they are not matters of wearing sandals, doing carpentry, or being celibate. Jesus taught that there is one specific way in which we are to be like him—the unconditional suffering love of the cross. "If any man would come after me, let him deny himself and take up his cross and follow me" (Mark 8:34). Peacemaking is costly and does not come easily. Yet that is the way to follow Jesus.

It is in our acceptance of the cross that we faithfully imitate Jesus, who is our model of nonviolent suffering love. "For to this you have been called, because Christ also suffered for you, leaving you an example, that you should follow in his steps" (1 Pet. 2:21). It is in love for enemies that we are godly. To be one with God, we must be like that child, a victim of the Khmer Rouge, who swore to get revenge by growing up and learning to love.

Yet how hard this is! I think of my old Chicago neighborhood. Our block had the dubious distinction of having two infamous street gangs, self-styled "gang-bangers."

Along with living on their turf came harassment, drug dealing, gun incidents, fighting, noise, tension, and fear. We worried about our safety and the vulnerability of children. The mere sight of certain gang kids could fill me with hate.

At best, I wished they would move. At worst, I had unmentionable fantasies. I wrote them off as evil enemies, unworthy of my love. I quickly forgot that they were themselves victims of racism, unemployment, and poverty. I, beneficiary of today's economic arrangements, was actually their enemy, not viceversa.

At times, they cursed and threatened me. Their swearing made me angry, even though I knew I had the benefits of the same system that condemned them. I needed to learn how to love. Booker T. Washington once said, "I will allow no people to drag me so low as to make me hate them." Would that we could all claim the same.

In a letter to Dorothy Day, Thomas Merton wrote, "For when we extend our hand to the enemy who is sinking in the abyss, God reaches out to both of us, for it is He first of all who extends our hand to the enemy."[13] Thus in Chicago I simply began to talk with the gang-bangers. When they broke laws, I often tried to speak with them rather than immediately call the police. Sometimes they continued to threaten me. But I was never touched, not even during the most tense encounters.

The threats sometimes took amazing directions. A gang member once walked uninvited into my yard at 3:00 a.m. His rumbling around near my house woke me. When I went outside he declared, "King Satan and I stand against everything you are trying to do." To this day, I have no idea what he meant.

In retrospect, I do not know whether my small initiatives made any improvements. Yet I know that before making them we certainly got nowhere. And I was pleased when the gang kids began to talk with me more and more, for—by their own admission—those conversations meant a loss of their power.

Will D. Campbell is a Baptist preacher from the South, long involved with the Civil Rights movement in the South. But one day he came to the startling realization that God loves everyone, including even the racists in the Ku Klux Klan. Thus, even as he continued his work for Civil Rights, Campbell went ahead and befriended people in the KKK.

He did this believing that God's reconciling love is for everyone. His KKK friends knew what he believed and what he stood for. But they also knew that he didn't write them off. Will Campbell did not consider them white trash. In a curious way, they respected and even loved each other.

Naive? Possibly. Idealistic? Perhaps. Unlikely? Of course! But the resurrection is all of these, as is God's merciful reconciliation. God does not work according to worldly projections and standards. Thank God. For the good news is that we are not trapped in old and tiresome realities.

Some years ago, the Grand Dragon of the North Carolina KKK, J. R. "Bob" Jones was indicted by the House Un-American Activities Committee (HUAC). He was not convicted of any crime except refusing to turn over the names of fellow members to HUAC. He was sentenced to a year in prison.

The night before Bob had to turn himself over for imprisonment, he had a party and invited Will Campbell. Before the end of the party, the Grand Dragon, who was brought up Lutheran, requested communion. Campbell preached in that KKK hotbed.

And now, as many as believe that a man can find his freedom in prison. As many as believe that no matter how blind, we can come to see. As many as believe that there is some way, somehow good news for the poor. As many as believe that the brokenhearted, those remaining at home, can be healed. Yes, as many as believe . . . that . . . Jesus . . . Christ . . . is Lord. Let them say hallelujah! And let them drink to, and let them drink of . . . His victory.[14]

Jones was sent to a prison that had a large group of militant black separatists. At first, the rumor in the black prison population was that the KKK Grand Dragon would be quickly assassinated. Some of Campbell's contacts persuaded the Black Muslims in the prison to protect Jones. There, Jones' best friend was his cellmate, a Black Muslim.

Unexpected liaisons and reconciliations across the boundaries of hate can bear unanticipated fruit, as in a tragic funeral after Jones was out of prison.

At the front of the line was the former Grand Dragon. By then he was out of prison and had resigned from the Klan. But instead of denouncing his neighbors and friends he denounced the war in Vietnam, because, he said, it was being fought by the poor, sons of his neighbors and friends. Black and white. Beside him was his Muslim prisonmate. Others included an Australian who was editing a magazine for an organization called Clergy and Laity Concerned About the War in Vietnam, a black United Methodist preacher, another Klansman, and others young and old, black and white, Catholic, Protestant, Jewish, and nothing. All under the canopy of a Roman Catholic cathedral in Summit, New Jersey.[15]

God's real and unlikely reconciliation shone here. It shone in the realignment of Jones' priorities. It shone through Jones and his new friends, the Black Muslims. Naive and idealistic and unlikely all. But the hardheaded and hardhearted souls who enmesh us in the nuclear arms race have only worse to offer.

"We beseech you on behalf of Christ, be reconciled to God" (2 Cor. 5:20b).

THIRTEEN

Fruits of Spirituality for Kingdom Workers

Actions That Bear Fruit

We saw that the prophets opposed religious rituals done in the context of injustice and oppression. Spiritual disciplines are not magical formulas that automatically win God's favor no matter how we live. Spirituality is inseparable from compassion. First Corinthians 13 reminds us of the primacy of love. "And if I have prophetic powers, and understand all mysteries and all knowledge, and if I have all faith, so as to remove mountains, but have not love, I am nothing" (v. 2).

True prayer involves, entails, and yields fruits of love, justice, and shalom that reveal God's kingdom. Without these, we are not dealing with biblical spirituality. Not everything labeled "prayer" is of value in and of itself. "Indeed, prayer must yield specific fruits. The final criterion of the value of the Christian life is therefore not prayer but action."[1]

We must be careful, however, when we suggest that prayer yields fruits or actions. This in itself does not mean that because prayer produces it is worthwhile. That again is a spiritualized version of that prevalent heresy which claims that something is worthwhile only when it gets results. So many of our understandings are seduced and distorted by worldly priorities. I recently heard a pastor describe church growth as being able to "design and deliver the product."

Christians act compassionately. Their compassionate works are an integral part and effect of their salvation. Yet neither their works nor fruits are what make them worthwhile. In the same way, true spirituality results in works of compassion. Although compassion is an integral part of spirituality—and the two cannot be separated—it is not the compassion that makes biblical spirituality valuable. The essential value of a person and the essential value of Christian spirituality is the source.

Humility

We do not pray because we are so good. We do not pray because we are perfect. We pray because we need to pray. We pray because we are weak and sinful. When not connected to God, we are less than nothing. Prayer is a confession of who we are and of our basic condition of need. In this sense, more prayer does not necessarily bring greater comfort and reassurance. On the contrary, more prayer brings greater vulnerability and further calls for conversion and repentance. Prayer's purpose is not to make us feel good.

Prayer is an act of repentance and humility. It does not give us cause for pride or self-congratulation. Rather, it perpetuates our conversion by convincing us of our continuing need to repent. "It unmasks the many illusions about ourselves and about God and leads us into the true relationship of the sinner to the merciful God."[2] Repentance, a central element in Jesus' teachings, is key to biblical spirituality.

The humility and repentance of prayer is integral to the witness of God's kingdom workers. Being Christ's ministers in an aching world, we are subject to many pharisaical delusions of self-righteousness. We work for God's kingdom and against all that opposes it not because we are good, but because we ourselves are evil.

We are constantly tempted to laud ourselves like the Pharisee: "God, I thank thee that I am not like other men, extortioners, unjust, adulterers, or even like this tax collector" (Luke 18:11). Instead of confessing our sins before God and others, we offer commercials about our worth.

Another aspect of our pride is pretending we are particularly important or effective. Yet this is not the way of Jesus. Being honest about our limitations and our sin, we frankly admit we are finite. Prayer helps us reach that crucial awareness of our weaknesses. "Prayer is . . . the inward cleanser of the distortions of action just as action is the clarifier and tester of prayer's real intent and of its genuine commitment."[3]

Hope and Persistence

The real hope, then, is not in something we think we can do, but in God who is making something good out of it in some way we cannot see. If we can do His will, we will be helping in this process. But we will not necessarily know all about it beforehand.[4]

Words about limitations and humility may discourage us. While admitting our weaknesses, we do well to remember other things as well. God is in control. Christ is Lord. Our God reigns. These are all a confession of the one true hope. There are other words to us besides the ones that remind us of the sin of all humanity.

Hope is a mystery we do not control. We cannot manipulate or create it. To pass through despair to hope is like going through the sea to dry land, or like dying on Friday and being born again on Sunday.

Ironically, despair is integral to hope. Optimism is the shallow avoidance of despair. Hope is not merely optimism because it is reached through—not around or over or in spite of—despair. Hope is a vision not confined or limited by what the world labels "feasible," "possible," or "realistic." This hopeful vision is grounded in our understanding of how God has worked in the past.

Further, the person of hope lives in the present, knowing that God works now, not only in the past or the future. Hope is the ability to be detached from specific results and to concentrate on doing good. Hope does not believe that the end justifies the means. When we are people of hope, then we can trust God's promises.

One February morning in 1987, a group of us huddled in the cold outside Chicago's United Methodist Temple. While the freezing Chicago wind bit us, we waited for a busload of

Freedom Riders. They were coming to help us organize and register voters in a crucial city election.

As I waited, I was not quite sure what to expect. I had come mostly as a favor to a friend. I felt sorry for myself. "I could be comfortably at home, keeping warm and drinking something hot!" Eventually, the bus arrived and out charged the enthusiastic Freedom Riders, wearing bright yellow T-shirts. From "down South," they didn't know how to dress in an "up South" Chicago winter.

Their bus had driven all night, but neither exhaustion nor cold slowed these folks. They came off the bus, rhythmically clapping and energetically singing, "Woke up this morning and my mind was stayed on Jesus!"

A shiver of joy went through us and our mood changed instantly. From cold and self-pitying, we became worshipful and cheery. Soon we were all singing. Even I was greatly moved, as suspicious as I always am of crowds and mass enthusiasm. My mind was stayed on Jesus. We were enlivened.

The book of Hebrews also talks of keeping one's mind stayed on Jesus: "Looking to Jesus the pioneer and perfecter of our faith, who for the joy that was set before him endured the cross, despising the shame, and is seated at the right hand of the throne of God" (Heb. 12:2).

Keeping our minds stayed on God's reality, paying attention to the deepest thing we know, our reality is changed, resurrected, and transfigured. "Now faith is the assurance of things hoped for, the conviction of things not seen" (Heb. 11:1). I like Clarence Jordan's translation of this verse. "Now faith is the turning of dreams into deeds; it is betting your life on the unseen realities."[5]

Faith then is not just agreeing intellectually with certain ideas. It involves not only our head and brains. Faith is more than saying, "I believe Jesus came, died, rose, ascended, and will come again."

Faith says, "I believe all that and therefore my life is changed. I believe all that and therefore the way I live in the world is affected. I believe all that and therefore I can wager my whole life on the reality of what Jesus did, is doing, and will do."

Faith is a conviction about the past and future that affects our present reality. Thus our lives are not only attuned to what our eyes see now. Rather, we also see what is ahead and promised. We do not confine ourselves to the present, but also embrace the future.

All of this reminds me of another Civil Rights song:

Keep your eyes on the prize.
Hold on.
Hold on.

For in keeping our eyes on God's prize, we can persist.

Now believing in unseen realities can get one in trouble, of course, as we see in the litany of Hebrews 11. Those faithful believers hung on and hung in. They were people who believed in God and God's promises enough to change and redirect their whole lives. For many, the price of their faith, the cost of their discipleship, was nothing less than great suffering and death.

Yet they persisted. Their eyes were on the prize. They were not deterred. "These all died in faith, not having received what was promised, but having seen it and greeted it from afar, and having acknowledged that they were strangers and exiles on the earth" (Heb. 11:13). These pilgrims had only the promises of God. And the promises were enough. Enough to get them by and see them through.

We who believe and confess our faith in Jesus Christ are the citizens of another kingdom. And although we work toward that kingdom here and now, we know we will not achieve it. Thus we are never completely at home here. We are "strangers and exiles on the earth . . . seeking a homeland" (Heb. 11:13b, 14b).

Nowadays, of course, the term otherworldly is greeted with suspicion. It is not politically correct. People do not want to be otherworldly. For many years, I was leery of any spirituality that might seem otherworldly. But otherworldliness is commended in Hebrews 11.

To be sure, there are forms of otherworldliness that are unhealthy, and unfaithful to the gospel. When I visited Haiti some years ago, I spent time speaking with Haitian Christians. Haiti is the poorest country in the Western hemisphere, yet has experienced and endured a glut of missions and development workers. There are well over two hundred development and missions organizations in a small nation with a population of about six million.

Haitian Christians complained to me about missionaries "who preach resignation and promise that someday we will have a nice palace." Throughout history, Christianity has been distorted to support oppression. Oppressors often claim the hereafter to perpetuate injustice on earth.

James Cone tells how a white slave owner tried to use other-worldly ideas to promote racism. The owner told the slave

> I dreamed I went to Nigger Heaven last night, and I saw there a lot of garbage, some torn-down houses, a few old broken down, rotten fences, the muddiest, sloppiest streets I ever saw, and a big bunch of ragged, dirty Negroes walking around.

But here false theology did not have the last word. The slave responded

> Umph, umph, Massa, . . . yah sho' musta et de same t'in Ah did las' night, 'cause Ah dreamed Ah went up ter de white man's paradise, an' de streets wuz all ob gol' and' silvah, and dey was lots o' milk an' honey dere, an' putty pearly gates, but dey wuzn't uh soul in de whole place."[6]

The otherworldliness of Old Testament believers was not neutral, oppressive, and uninvolved. Otherwise, they could have stayed in one place. But they affected their surrounding cultures. They made a difference. Abraham and Sarah were the parents of a new nation. Moses collaborated with God in liberating the slaves from Egypt. The examples go on and on.

Thus otherworldliness in itself is not necessarily bad or good. Bad otherworldliness is when we are not concerned about our neighbors in this world. Likewise, there can be bad forms of this-worldliness. People can become so preoccupied with this world and its meager rewards that they lose the important perspective.

In 1987, political pundits marveled at the success of Canada's socialist New Democratic Party (NDP) in three by-elections. People wondered whether the NDP could ever gain a majority in the federal Parliament. Analysts predicted that since the NDP might be close to power, it would sacrifice some of its ideals and commitments. It would no longer be so outspoken about the issues that separated it from the other parties. Suddenly NDP rhetoric would become cautious and restrained. NDP politicians would sacrifice their uniqueness to gain power. By the time they gained power (if they succeeded), they would not be distinguishable from the other political parties.

Christians often make the mistake of valuing power over platform. We need always to remember that what we are striving for will be in the future and is promised to us. We must understand from Hebrews 11 that we can never be at home here on earth. As soon as we think we can achieve control and possibly the kingdom, we are suddenly willing to make unfortunate compromises or take shortcuts.

Many Christians get totally involved in a cause. There's nothing wrong with that, as Christians ought to be highly committed. But we also must remember God's bigger picture. For many Christians also burn out, give up, and despair just because of relatively small defeats.

Hebrews 11 reminds us of the vision, the hope, the prize, and the faith that is ours. For when we keep God's perspective, then we can persist and hope. God's future prize enables us today. In discussing the hope of black slaves, Cone notes, "The future becomes a present reality in the slave's consciousness, enabling him to struggle against the white system of injustice."[7]

Keeping our eyes on God's prize, hoping for God's reality, carries us to places that our willpower alone cannot reach. In Chicago, one of my favorite parishioners was an elderly, widowed shut-in, named Ann. She had been chronically ill for fourteen years. I visited her regularly as part of my ministry, but the truth is that she ministered to me.

No matter how poorly she felt, Ann rose early every day. She took good care of herself. She was not allowed by her doctor to go outside, but she stood in her door and talked to the neighbors. She prayed for many people and scrawled out countless notes of encouragement to all and sundry. She always had a sense of humor, a smile, and a prayer for others, despite constant pain. Her faith saw her through.

When Ann died, her body was worn out; her time had come. Her life, in spite of brokenness and pain, was a triumph. Hers was no ordinary funeral. We pastors who served in the funeral could not keep a professionally calm demeanor. We cried at her passing because we missed her. Her presence was a help and support.

Because of her faith, Ann saw beyond her pain, helping those around her. She taught me much about what it means to keep your eyes on the prize and hold on, hold on.

Be Still and Know That I Am God

We live in a world of insecurity. One has only to open a news-paper to find many reasons for despair. Environmental problems (acid rain, depletion of the ozone layer, and global warming) plague our earth. We are faced with massive threats to life, nuclear weapons, and AIDS. Strangely and mysteriously, the Bible recommends that in the midst of all this turmoil we should trust God and be secure.

Several times now, we have reflected on the meaning of Im-manuel, God-with-us, for our spirituality. As it turns out, the original Immanuel-promise was offered at a time when people believed that their civilization was in full danger of being de-stroyed.

In Isaiah 6, we read the famous account of Isaiah's call to be a prophet. "I saw the Lord sitting upon a throne, high and lifted up; and his train filled the temple" (6:1). That mystical ex-perience did not leave him in ecstasy, however. Rather, it led him away from the temple to a political confrontation.

He moved from the majestic vision of the true King to conflict with a human king, Ahaz. Because of the perspective gained through his prayers, Isaiah was immersed in a conflict between divine politics and human politics.

Isaiah 7 tells of a crisis that faced the nation of Judah, a crisis that some believed would end civilization as they knew it. It seemed that Jerusalem, with its magnificent temple, might fall into the hands of heathens.

Israel and Syria were allied in war against Judah. They demanded that Judah join the alliance. To secure their request, they attacked Judah. In response to the threat, the king's "heart and the heart of his people shook as the trees of the forest shake before the wind" (Isa. 7:2b).

Biblical authors did not look favorably on King Ahaz. "And he did not do what was right in the eyes of the Lord his God, as his father David had done . . ." (2 Kings 16:2b). Specifically, he was an idolater; "he sacrificed and burned incense on the high places, and on the hills, and under every green tree" (2 Kings 16:4).

Most appallingly, "He even burned his son as an offering, according to the abominable practices of the nations whom the Lord drove out before the people of Israel" (2 Kings 16:3b). Not surprisingly, this king intended to appeal to pagan Assyria for help against Syria and Israel. To seal the alliance, he would even give silver and gold from the temple to Assyria.

Isaiah was dragged by God into this tense political situation. He was to meet Ahaz "at the end of the conduit of the upper pool on the highway to the Fuller's Field . . ." (Isa. 7:3b). The king was apparently checking the water supply, ensuring that Jerusalem could have enough water to withstand a siege.

While Ahaz was engaged in such strategic military preparations, Isaiah brought this unlikely advice: "Take heed, be quiet, do not fear, and do not let your heart be faint . . ." (Isa. 7:4a). Not exactly hard-nosed geopolitical strategy, and Ahaz would disregard it.

Isaiah's advice was based on at least two understandings. One, the Syrian-Israelite alliance was extremely weak, "two smoldering stumps of firebrands" (7:4). In fact, Israel would eventually be destroyed (7:8). Rather than allying with Assyria, or joining with Syria and Israel, Isaiah suggested that Ahaz resist all the warring parties and count on God alone.

But Isaiah was not only being politically realistic. Ahaz was a typical king, striving to control history. Isaiah reminded Ahaz that God was the true King, in charge of the world. No one could stand without God. "If you will not believe, surely you shall not be established" (Isa. 7:9b).

In spite of the biblical soundness of his assertions, Isaiah offered Ahaz a sign of God's power, "let it be deep as Sheol or high as heaven." (Isa. 7:11b). But Ahaz, the idolater, suddenly turned pious. "I will not ask, and I will not put the Lord to the test" (Isa. 7:12).

One might almost mistake Ahaz's dismissal as faithfulness. After all, Jesus similarly resisted a sign when he was tempted in the wilderness. "You shall not tempt the Lord your God" (Matt. 4:7). But there was a difference: here God made an offer Ahaz spurned.

Jesus did not need a sign because he trusted God. Ahaz refused God's offer of a sign, because nothing would convince him to trust God. He reminds me of a T-shirt I see from time to time: "My mind's made up, don't confuse me with the facts."

In spite of Ahaz's obstinacy, God graciously gave a sign. "Behold, a young woman shall conceive and bear a son, and shall call his name Immanuel" (Isa. 7:14). Matthew believed this promise referred to Jesus (Matt. 1:23). The name means "God with us." In the midst of a catastrophic political crisis, God gave this sign of hope and joy. Because of God's hope, Isaiah did not despair or surrender even in the worst of circumstances.

Such hopes have bolstered God's faithful people throughout history. While we may think our world is near its end (it may well be), we are not the first generation to believe so.

Christian hope and joy is not rooted in optimism, affluence, or success. In the Bible, we find few believers who are extremely successful. Christian hope comes from a conviction about God's loving involvement with us in our lives and various circumstances.

Psalm 46 teaches what it means to trust God. This psalm has an Immanuel-like refrain:

> The Lord of hosts is with us;
> the God of Jacob is our refuge (46:7, 11).

The psalmist offers us encouraging words.

> God is our refuge and strength,
> a very present help in trouble (46:1).

But note this and note this well: God's refuge, strength and help comes in the midst of trouble. And troubles there are aplenty. A changing earth and shaking sea mountains (46:2). Roaring waters and trembling mountains (46:3). Raging nations, tottering kingdoms, and a melting earth (46:6). Thus God's reassurance and help is paradoxical, coming to us and being present with us at the worst of times. Likewise, the believer's life is lived in the midst of paradox.

Visiting the park with my children is itself a study in contradictions, mysteries, and enigmas. The three of us often walk through the high society section of Windsor's Walkerville neighborhood. Walkerville is named for its first benefactor, Hiram Walker of Canadian Club Whiskey fame.

As we stroll along, we often gawk at the mansions that some choose to live in. But even as we do so, I cannot help remembering that the neighborhood was largely built by whiskey. And more than that, much of Walkerville's money came from bootlegging and rum-running during the Prohibition era. So, for all its propriety and feigned sobriety, the neighborhood has unseemly beginnings.

The object of the stroll is Willistead Park, once the estate of the Walker family. In the middle of the estate sits a huge gray stone mansion with Tudor gables. It is the scene of high teas and gaudily attired wedding parties. It was originally built for the decadent ostentation of a wealthy family and financed by whiskey. Now it is a public park that is shared by all.

In its green acres, one finds towering oaks and tall maples. Although carefully managed and manicured, it remains a small reminder of God's vast creation. While children peacefully play with one another, a police officer regularly wanders through. She smiles at the children and chats pleasantly with them.

At the same time, she eyes the adults suspiciously. It seems the area has been plagued with a flasher. The park is filled with contradictions and paradoxes.

For our travels, we have a wobbly old heap of a stroller. When our first child was due, someone gave us a stroller that we quickly wore out. I found this second stroller in a ghetto alley in Chicago. Ironically, that cast-off serves us better than the stroller given to us as a gift.

Nevertheless, the stroller provides an adventurous ride. It shakes and rattles, wobbling away and every second threatening to fall into a disorderly heap of plastic and bolts. It you take the stroller on a reasonable sidewalk, it makes its way well enough— although its suspension is nonexistent and its alignment a farce.

Should you decide to drive the stroller over a lawn, you really have to work. For the little bumps and hillocks of a lawn are a terrific obstacle to that rattletrap. One has to force, push, jerk, and shove it to get it and keep it moving.

One day, the kids wanted me to cut across the vast lawn in a shortcut from an intersection of sidewalks to the all-important playground. But we did not discover the shortcut. Dozens, possibly hundreds, of bikes had made it over the years. Their wheels had cut a narrow path, no more than three inches across, etched like a shining line through the green and uneven grass.

Even though the stroller is almost impossible to push over the lumpy lawn, my two-year-old insisted on riding. He had no intention of walking across the couple acres on his own feet. I complied. I pushed the stroller with two of its wheels on the narrow path and two riding the lawn. This was not smooth, but shaky. Yet it was surer and more steady than just riding on the grass.

And so in our life.

Even today we move between two worlds—the temporal present and the eternal now. Our feet, our wheels if you will, are planted between two realities. They are on the lumpy uncertainty of God's earth and on God's straight and narrow path.

Our path as Christians is not always as sure as that cut in Willistead Park by bicyclists. But we do have the heritage and legacy of faithful folk who have traversed this world before us. And of course we have God's word to guide us. As sure as that path through the lawn, we can trust that God is with us.

The route is sometimes shaky. Our alignment is often out of whack. Outside forces assail us. But God's path is sure.

Timid Faithfulness

Thou dost keep him in perfect peace,
whose mind is stayed on thee,
because he trusts in thee.
Trust in the Lord for ever,

for the Lord God
is an everlasting rock (Isa. 26:3-4).

One election day, November 6. 1984, will always be prominent in my memory. I was one of four Mennonite staff who accompanied eight students from an alternative high school in Chicago to the Great Lakes Naval Base. We went to express our concern about the increasing militarization of the United States and the looming possibility of an invasion of Central America. Although we were only twelve people, with two little signs, the town swarmed with dozens of police and naval security personnel. We were followed everywhere.

We quietly walked to a public vacant lot visible to those entering the base. We silently held up simple signs that read, in English and Spanish, "Let us live in peace." A nearby billboard read, "Christian Serviceman's Center: Jesus Is Coming Soon."

Within minutes, police officers warned us against "demonstrating without a permit." They threatened to arrest us no matter what we did—whether we walked in a group or pairs or singly in town, with or without signs. All this even though the law said that it takes at least fifty or more people to demonstrate without a permit.

Returning to our cars, we discussed the situation. "Where are we?" one student asked. Where indeed? Surely not in a land that respects freedom of speech and assembly. Not wanting the students arrested, two staff took them away.

But two of us remained. For us, it was not just an issue of rights. It was a matter of duty and faithfulness. We wanted to testify to our faith, which calls us to witness for a new kingdom. "We must obey God rather than people." Law enforcers oversaw Jesus' crucifixion and law enforcers tried to cover up the resurrection. Thus threats of arrest should not deter us from faithful witness. Although scared, we returned to the vacant lot with our signs.

Within minutes, we were arrested, handcuffed, and dragged to the paddy wagon. As the paddy wagon bounced over the rough road, and as I vainly sought to stay securely on the metal bench, my hands bound behind me, I wondered if I had made a terrible mistake. And I knew that now there was no way out.

At the police station, four officers carried me out of the paddy wagon. They twisted my arms twisted over my head, jamming my body into each hall corner. I was hurt enough that I wanted to walk. But the officers joked about my attempt and kept dragging me around.

Our ten friends lingered nearby, concerned for us. Followed by a paddy wagon and plainclothes police, they were told to keep moving. The police even followed them into a restaurant. Vehicles tailed them out of town and through two suburbs.

While being booked, I heard police radio in about suspicious "protest" vehicles in town. Their paranoia had the better of them. Our friends had left. After spending some hours in a holding cell, we were released and given an arraignment date.

This arrest and the subsequent trial were among the worst experiences in my life. While risking the arrest, I knew that my wife might soon go into labor with our first child. I did not want her to experience that alone. Yet in my protest I acted for our child and for all children.

I wondered whether I was being a poor father. Was not my prime duty at home, especially as my first child's life was about to be born? I was frustrated, wondering why we could not have a secure parenting experience. I resented the forces that dragged me into such risky involvements. But even as we endured the terrible experience of a trial and conviction, our life was graced with the arrival of Erin, one of the happiest events in our life.

As a chronic worrier, the imagined possibilities overwhelmed me. Jesus told us to take up our crosses and follow him. I cannot face all the crosses in my future, but God doesn't require me to carry 365 crosses at once. I carry only one day's cross at a time. "Therefore do not be anxious about tomorrow, for tomorrow will be anxious for itself. Let the day's own trouble be sufficient for the day" (Matt. 6:34).

God cares for and protects us more than we ever understand. Indeed, "even the hairs of your head are numbered. Fear not, therefore; you are of more value than many sparrows" (Matt. 10:30-31). Jesus gave this assurance even while he warned the disciples of arrests and persecutions.

With my seminary education, I blithely preach God's promises. Words are easy. But God's words have proven true for me over and again. God's grace has brought me far. God continually calls us to greater faithfulness, and I know with God's help it is possible.

FOURTEEN

Parting Vignettes

The Courtesy of Being Prayerful

When I was a child, my mother often told a story from her own childhood. Her family was from rural Friesland, in the northern Netherlands. They did not learn all the ins and outs of etiquette observed by people in town. One year, my mother was invited to a birthday party of a school chum in town. This was an exciting occasion for her. Added to this pleasure was the good news that the birthday supper was pancakes, one of my mother's favorite foods.

The pancakes were thin and floppy crepes. When my mother received her first pancake, she rolled it up with her fingers and began eating with both her hands—just the way that they always ate pancakes at home. The other children laughed. They were eating their pancakes properly with knife and fork. My mother had never learned how. Absolutely mortified, she made an important resolution. *When I grow up, I will teach my children to eat with a fork and knife.*

She tried to do just that. And although I have not proven the most able etiquette student, I at least know how to eat with a knife and fork when so inclined. I often resented it when my mother tried to teach me manners. It seemed an infringement on my liberty, an imposition, an inconvenience, an unnatural obstacle.

But I eventually understood her story. She had taught me manners so that I would know how to use them (and because she wants me to be polite). I could choose to be impolite but I also would know how to behave properly and not be embarrassed. The discipline of learning apparently silly rules and regimens actually frees me to behave comfortably in a variety of settings.

That makes even more sense to me now as a parent. My generation puts less emphasis on etiquette for children; I appreciate some of the concerns about not stifling children; my children are freer than I was. Nevertheless I insist they learn basic manners. In the long run, they will be better off if they know how to be polite. For now, it is also important for them to acknowledge their dependence on others and act respectfully, rather than just demanding things. Parents also need and deserve to feel some respect and appreciation from children. In King Lear, Shakespeare wrote:

"How sharper than a serpent's tooth it is
to have a thankless child!"

Adults likewise need to be polite to children, being respectful and modeling ways they expect children to live.

The way we train small children in politeness is straightforward. When they ask for something, we ask, "What do you say?" But "please" is not enough. They are also to include the adult's name or title. Similarly, if we give them something and hear no response, we ask, "What do you say?" And we wait for a "thank you."

Children soon sense that politeness allows some room for manipulation. If one is impolite, one will probably not get what one desires. However, if one is polite the odds are a little better.

Inevitably, conflicts arise when the children ask for something that we have no intention of giving them. At such times, they even resort to pleading pleases. "Pleeease, pleeease, pleeease!" But politeness and magic words are not enough to guarantee the granting of their request. If they ask for something that will be bad for them, no amount of pleases will get their way. I remember the surprised disillusion as both my children first learned this hard lesson.

On the other hand, my children are guaranteed certain things whether or not they are polite. We will unconditionally feed them, clothe them, shelter them, protect them, teach them. We give them what they need, always hoping they will receive it politely, but delivering it even when they are rude.

There are also times we give to them even when they are rude. If one is sick with a fever and brusquely asks for a drink, that is not the time to train a junior Miss or Mister Manners. Then we give because their basic needs are crucial. And often I give them what they need long before they ask for it, since they do not even understand their own needs as I do.

I am more and more convinced that the teaching of manners to my children is parallel to a life of prayer. It is strange that in our day we must persuade people to pray. We need to prove to them that they will get something out of their prayers. Is it not enough to say that God desires us to pray, asks us to pray? What more do we need to know?

When we say grace before our meals, we ask God's blessing as well as give thanks for God's providence. There is no better reason to pray than that God desires it. It is the least we can do. It is the essence of good manners before God. Yet how often we are rude before God!

> And as he entered a village, he was met by ten lepers, who stood at a distance and lifted up their voices and said, 'Jesus, Master, have mercy on us.' When he saw them he said to them, 'Go and show yourselves to the priests.' And as they went they were cleansed. Then one of them, when he saw that he was healed, turned back, praising God with a loud voice; and he fell on his face at Jesus' feet, giving him thanks. Now he was a Samaritan. Then said Jesus, 'Were not ten cleansed? Where are the nine? Was no one found to return and give praise to God except this foreigner?' And he said to him, 'Rise and go your way; your faith has made you well' " (Luke 17:12-19).

That story is an accurate reflection of our society's ingratitude before the holy one. Notice that all the lepers were healed, even though only one was polite. That resembles the reality that a parent cares for even rude children. "If you then, who are evil, know how to give good gifts to your children, how much more will your Father who is in heaven give good things to those who ask him!" (Matt. 7:11).

Which brings us to another point. The Samaritan, aware of what God through Jesus had done, responded with worship. (I almost wrote that he responded that way "naturally," but am uncertain of whether he or his nine co-sufferers were acting more or less naturally.) His response was a free one—"praising God with a loud voice." He did not praise to receive anything else.

Jesus' blessing of being "well" (or "whole") was a bonus. We can make only one appropriate response, we who have been saved from the powers of this dark age, have been rebirthed into God's kingdom, have no need to fear death, have already begun to experience the promise of the resurrection. That response is to live grateful lives of praise and so to become more fully well and whole.

We have examined the heresies of those who believe that prayer is magic which will gain them privileges and perks, such as health and wealth. The truth is that we have already gained more than we deserve. God will not be manipulated by our prayers (much less than I am manipulated by my children's good manners . . . if and when they are polite). Likewise, God showered me with redemptive blessings long before I understood what God was about, long before I was polite. Like a good parent, God is attentive to us not only when we bother to call for help.

We do not pray because God will bless us. We do not pray because it will make us feel good. We do not pray because it will make us feel better. We pray because God recommends, desires, and demands it. And God knows what we need and what our relationship with God requires.

I know all too many people who quickly give up on prayer because they have not experienced a rush, a high, a sense of consolation, and reassurance. There are simply no guarantees in prayer—except that it works in unexpected ways.

In fact, I daresay that prayer's unexpected results will make us uncomfortable. Michael Schwartzentruber suffers from cystic fi-

brosis and describes the procedures he must follow just to survive. As well as taking certain medications, his body daily needs
to be physically pounded to clear it of life-threatening mucus.

> I have a padded board which can be set up [at] various angles, one
> end on the floor, the other end raised. I lie on this board in five dif-
> ferent positions, most of them head down. In each position, Jan hits,
> with a cupped hand, a different area of my chest. The internal vibra-
> tion looses the mucus in that area of the lung. After each position, I
> must sit up and cough out the mucus.[1]

The procedure is time-consuming and painful. It does not
necessarily make Michael feel better. It does not even heal him.
But it is crucial.

The same is true of prayer. It needs to be done regularly. It is
the way to live faithfully. Only through such disciplines do we
allow God to clear out the mucus that gathers so quickly in our
hearts and lives. It may be rough, uncomfortable, and unwieldy
—as Michael's therapy most certainly is—but it is just as essential
and crucial.

Sister Mary Jo Leddy wrote a beautiful book about her parents' experience during World War II, *Memories of War: Promises
of Peace*. In it she describes the horrors and suffering that her
father, Jack, endured as an Allied military surgeon working near
the battle lines of France. One of his consolations at that time
was a little church. It

> was one of the few buildings that had been left standing after a mas-
> sive bombardment. Sunday services were held there—the Catholic
> and Protestant services scheduled at different times. Many of the
> men went to the services but weren't too concerned which one they
> attended. Jack would go down to the church for a few minutes when
> he was not on duty. It became his place of refuge.[2]

There he could think about loved ones, remember his fallen
friends, process his terrible war memories, relax, and pray. Years
later, he returned to Europe with his wife and daughters, insist-
ing that they visit this precious place. He had often told them
what an important place this was for him.

When we reached the church Dad was delighted and wanted to go inside right away. The rest of us were reduced to silence until my mother finally said what my sister and I were already thinking: "My God, it's ugly."

Ugly was the word. The walls were beige stones stained and covered with fungus. On the roof was something that looked more like a chimney than a bell tower. In any case, there was no bell to ring. Not a single flower or blade of grass grew in the grim clay ground around.[3]

As wife and daughters marveled at the ugliness of the church, Jack tried to recover from his surprise and hurt. "Dad looked at us blankly. In 1944, he had never really noticed what the church looked like. 'It looked pretty good at the time,' he said. 'It was a place to go and pray.'"[4]

Jack had been blessed when he met God where God was prepared to meet him. "This was where he was at home in the world, where he knew who he was with God. He was far more at home there than in all the nice churches he would attend on Sundays in his later life."[5]

When God encounters us, it is often in ways that are unexpected and unsettling, possibly even ugly or repulsive to those on the outside. But to encounter God, walk with God, keep company with God, we must respect God's terms. Had Jack had the option of being a church shopper during World War II, he probably would not have chosen the little church that helped nourish him. And he would have been the loser.

Philip Amerson writes about a visit to a New England retreat center. Near the dining hall, a huge bell was suspended in a low wooden frame. People were continually tempted to make that bell ring. "We had tapped, pounded, and otherwise tested the outer sound bow of the great old retired chime salvaged from a razed Congregational church nearby."[6]

But it was all to no avail. "Each time the bell was struck, disappointment struck. A bland, muffled gong was all it seemed able to muster." Neither hands nor stones were able to elicit a chime from the bell. All week long, the bell tempted and teased each and every passerby, but it never released its fruit. "Tuneless, no wonder the old fellow had been set aside. It was, we were now certain, a shapely but ignoble discard."

Eventually someone told the grounds keeper of their frustration. He said nothing but smiled. He left momentarily and returned with a ball peen hammer. He moved to the bell, put his arm within, and struck three times.

> The evening was transformed. Three honey sweet, resonate peals swelled across the yard and out beyond the alfalfa fields and down the road. Echoes were awakened in the evening breezes and in our memories. Such reverberating beauty, like a magnificent Angelus greeting the incarnation. We applauded. All of us would-be bell ringers were struck by the power of the moment. How it stirred us! The grounds keeper was the carillonneur. He knew the secret. He knew the obvious. To hear the chime, the bell needed to be struck from the inside.

Prayer reminds us that we cannot ring our own bell. Relying on God, we stop dinging ourselves on the outside with worries, anxiety, dissipation, and compulsions. Prayer helps us stop long enough so that God can reach deep inside us and strike surely the chimes of our heart, releasing sweet peals of music.

Some time ago, I heard an interesting lecture on falconry. I was fascinated by how owners tame their hawks. A crucial aspect of the training is for the trainer to keep a bird on his or her hand during all waking hours. This helps trainer and falcon grow accustomed to one another. At the same time, the trainer keeps food in one hand. There is a specific moment the trainer awaits—the time the bird takes the food from the trainer's hand. This is important because the bird must bend down and turn its eyes away from the trainer. Now, the bird can no longer watch suspiciously and distrustfully. This goes against the bird's deepest instincts.

This is much like our relationship to God. God tries to teach and tame us, to build us up, to rework us. But we are so resistant, so proud, so suspicious, so protective. In prayer, we keep company with God. Slowly our defenses against God dissolve.

God waits for our bent knees. When will we avert our suspicious eyes and act in humility, obedience, and innocence? That is what we do when we bend the knee in baptism. That is what we do when we bow our head and take communion. We submit ourselves to God's will, God's way, God's work. We say not our will but yours be done on earth as in heaven.

Notes

Introduction

1. Eugene H. Peterson, *Working the Angles* (Grand Rapids: William B. Eerdmans Publishing Company, 1987), p. 2.

Chapter One

1. Simone Weil, *Waiting for God*, trans. Emma Craufurd (New York: Harper & Row, 1951), p. 69.

2. Ibid., p. 105.

3. Ann Marie Rousseau, *Shopping Bag Ladies* (New York: The Pilgrim Press, 1981), p. 10.

4. Abraham Kuyper as quoted in *Space for God*, by Don Postema (Grand Rapids: Bible Way, 1983), p. 99.

5. The word *dwell* in "Hebrew suggests impermanence and is better translated by the word 'tent.' God lives in the heavens, but He 'tents' among His people, a concept used later by a Gospel writer concerning the incarnation (John 1.14)." Millard C. Lind, *Biblical Foundations of Christian Worship* (Scottdale: Herald Press, 1973), p. 19.

Chapter Two

1. This information about the international debt and these quotes are from Keith Gingrich, "MCC Helps Bring Africans to Discuss Third World Debt," *The Mennonite*, April 1989, p. 158.

Chapter Three

1. Quoted in the photograph exhibit, *Gifts of War*, by Larry Towell.

2. This story and its quotes are from Jim Wallis, "The Second Reformation Has Begun," *Sojourners*, January 1990, p. 16.

3. Dean Peerman, "El Salvador's Beleaguered Lutheran Bishop" *Christian Century*, January 31, 1990, p. 94.

Chapter Four

1. "The clans at Sinai needed no command to sacrifice. They and their fathers had done this from primitive times. . . . [Sacrifice] was not at all central to biblical faith, but was a cultural item too intimately tied to human existence to be immediately rejected." Millard C. Lind, *Biblical Foundations of Christian Worship* (Scottdale: Herald Press, 1973), p. 16.

2. Rafael Avila, *Worship and Politics*, trans. Alan Neely (Maryknoll: Orbis Books, 1981), p. 27.

3. Ibid., pp. 20-23.

4. Frederick Buechner, *Wishful Thinking* (New York: Harper & Row, 1973), p. 55.

5. *The Journals of Kierkegaard*, trans. and ed. by Alexander Dru (New York: Harper Torchbooks, 1959), p. 97.

6. E. Stanley Jones as quoted in *Liberating Ministry from the Success Syndrome* by Kent and Barbara Hughes (Wheaton: Tyndale, 1988), p. 73.

7. Clarence Jordan and Bill Lane Doulos, *Cotton Patch Parables of Liberation* (Scottdale: Herald Press, 1976), p. 94.

Chapter Five

1. William Stringfellow, *An Ethic for Christians and Other Aliens in a Strange Land* (Waco: Word Books, 1973), p. 15.

2. Millard C. Lind in *Biblical Foundations of Christian Worship* (Scottdale: Herald Press, 1973), p. 38.

3. Ibid., p. 39.

4. Ibid., p. 5.

5. Ibid., p. 10.

6. Ibid., p. 11.

7. Ibid., p. 17.

8. For example, Ps. 10:16; 93; 96; 97; 98; 99; 146; Isa. 52:7.

9. Lind, *Worship*, pp. 11-36.

10. Ibid., p. 21.

11. Ibid., p. 38.

12. "That Christ is Lord, a proclamation to which only individuals can respond, is nonetheless a social, political, structural fact which constitutes a challenge to the Powers." John Howard Yoder, *The Politics of Jesus* (Grand Rapids: William B. Eerdmans Publishing Company, 1972), pp. 160-161.

13. The Lord's Prayer "is a prayer not of an individual but of a people, whose sense of peoplehood is expressed in the plural pronouns 'our' and 'us.' It is the corporate prayer of a people whose first concern is not for themselves but for the political leadership of God in the world. . . ." Lind, *Worship*, p. 40.

14. William Stringfellow, *Instead of Jesus* (New York: The Seabury Press, 1976), p. 6.

15. Lind, *Worship*, p. 45.

16. Ibid., p. 28.

17. Soren Kierkegaard, *Works of Love*, trans. Howard and Edna Hong (New York: Harper & Row, Publishers, 1962), p. 84.

18. Lind, *Worship*, p. 50.

19. Allan A. Boesak, *Comfort and Protest: The Apocalypse from a South African Perspective* (Philadelphia: The Westminster Press, 1987), p. 137.

20. Ibid., p. 17.

21. John E. Burkhart, *Worship* (Philadelphia: The Westminster Press, 1982), p. 17.

22. Lind, *Worship*, p. 5.

23. This quote and story are from Will D. Campbell's Foreword in *Into the Darkness* by Gene L. Davenport (Nashville: Abingdon Press, 1989), p. 10.

24. "It is a mistake to regard Christian worship primarily as individual piety. . . ." Lind, *Worship*, p. 38.

25. Lind, *Worship*, p. 56.

26. James H. Cone, *God of the Oppressed* (New York: The Seabury Press, 1975), p. 144.

27. Richard Mouw, "Being with the Lamb," *Sojourners*, March 1981, p. 22.

Chapter Six

1. Frederick Buechner, *Wishful Thinking* (New York: Harper & Row, 1973), p. 24.

Introduction to Part Two

1. Frederick Buechner, *The Hungering Dark* (New York: The Seabury Press, 1969), pp. 73-74.

Chapter Seven

1. Frederick Buechner, *The Hungering Dark* (New York: The Seabury Press, 1969), p. 74.

2. Ibid., p. 75.

3. Frederick Buechner, *Wishful Thinking* (New York: Harper & Row, 1973), p. 94.

4. Jacques Ellul, *The Politics of God and the Politics of Man*, trans. Geoffrey W. Bromiley (Grand Rapids: William B. Eerdmans Publishing Company, 1972), pp. 192-193.

5. Jacques Ellul, *Prayer and Modern Man*, trans. C. Edward Hopkin (New York: The Seabury Press, 1970), p. 139.

6. Ibid., p. 62.

7. Soren Kierkegaard, *Works of Love*, trans. Howard and Edna Hong (New York: Harper & Row, Publishers, 1962), p. 108.

8. Eugene H. Peterson, *Answering God* (New York: Harper & Row, 1989), p. 54.

9. Simone Weil, *Waiting for God*, trans. Emma Craufurd (New York: Harper & Row, 1951), p. 69.

10. Henri J. M. Nouwen, *Making All Things New* (New York: Harper & Row, Publishers, 1981), p. 66.

11. Nouwen, *Reaching Out* (Garden City: Doubleday & Company, Inc., 1975), p. 88.

12. Soren Kierkegaard, *Training in Christianity* (Princeton: Princeton University Press, 1967), p. 30.

13. Soren Kierkegaard, *Attack Upon Christendom*, trans. Walter Lowrie (Princeton: Princeton University Press, 1968), p. 219.

Chapter Eight

1. Georgia Harkness, *The Providence of God* (Nashville: Abingdon Press, 1960).

2. Ibid., p. 17.

3. *The Heidelberg Catechism* (Philadelphia: United Church Press, 1962), Question 26, p. 31.

4. Ibid., Question 26, p. 31.

5. Ibid., Question 26, p. 31.

6. As quoted in *The Oxford Dictionary of Quotations, Third Edition* (New York: Oxford University Press, 1979), p. 532.

7. E. Glenn Hinson, "A Minister's Devotional Life," in *Pulpit Digest*, March/April 1989, p. 69.

8. Ibid., pp. 70-71.

9. Harkness, *Providence*, p. 43.

10. Ibid., p. 46.

Chapter Nine

1. Michel Quoist, *Prayers*, trans. Agnes M. Forsyth and Anne Marie de Commaille (New York: Sheed and Ward, 1963), p. 17.

2. Ibid., p. 1.

3. Ibid., p. 29.

4. *The Book of Common Prayer* (New York: The Seabury Press, 1979), p. 302.

5. Søren Kierkegaard, *The Works of Love,* trans. Howard and Edna Hong (New York: Harper & Row, Publishers, 1962), p. 105.

6. John Howard Yoder, *The Politics of Jesus* (Grand Rapids: Eerdmans, 1972), p. 238.

7. Frederick Buechner, *The Magnificent Defeat* (New York: The Seabury Press, 1966), p. 18.

8. Brother Lawrence, *The Practice of the Presence of God* (Old Tappan, New Jersey: Fleming H. Revell Company, 1958), p. 27.

9. Ibid., p. 18.

10. Ibid., p. 29.

11. Buechner, *The Hungering Dark,* p. 24.

12. Soren Kierkegaard, "Concluding Unscientific Postscript to the Philosophical Fragments," trans. David F. Swenson, Lillian Marvin Swenson, and Walter Lowrie in *A Kierkegaard Anthology,* ed. Robert Brettall (New York: The Modern Library, 1946), p. 225.

Chapter Ten

1. Douglas V. Steere, *Together in Solitude* (New York: Crossroad, 1982), p. 25.

2. Anonymous, The Way of a Pilgrim, trans. R. M. French (London: SPCK, 1960).

3. Ibid., p. 9.

4. Henri J. M. Nouwen, *The Way of the Heart* (New York: Seabury, 1981), p. 81.

5. Ibid., pp. 82-83.

6. Don Postema, *Space for God* (Grand Rapids: Bible Way, 1983), p. 113.

7. Sheila Cassidy, *Audacity to Believe* (London: Collins, 1977), p. 210.

8. Ibid., pp. 222-223.

9. Anthony Bloom, *Beginning to Pray* (New York: Paulist Press, 1970), p. 5.

10. Thomas Merton, *Thoughts in Solitude* (New York: Farrar, Straus and Giroux, 1977), p. 105.

11. Nouwen, *With Open Hands,* 86.

12. Frederick Buechner, *Godric* (New York: Atheneum, 1980), p. 142.

13. Walter Wink, *Unmasking the Powers* (Philadelphia: Fortress Press, 1986), p. 91.

14. Clarence Jordan and Bill Lane Doulos, *Cotton Patch Parables of Liberation* (Scottdale: Herald Press, 1976), p. 83. The book further notes: "The word translated 'nags' is a graphic word in the Greek with a violent physical connotation. The verb form literally means 'to beat black and blue.' Perhaps this widow brought her cane to the courthouse!"

15. Abraham J. Heschel, *The Prophets,* vol. II (New York: Harper & Row, Publishers, 1962), pp. 64-65.

16. Abraham J. Heschel, *The Prophets,* vol. I (New York: Harper & Row, Publishers, 1962), pp. 204-205.

Chapter Eleven

1. Michel Quoist, *I've Met Jesus Christ,* trans. J. F. Bernard (New York: Image Books, 1975), p. 128.

2. Jacques Ellul, *Prayer and the Modern Man,* trans. C. Edward Hopkin (New York: The Seabury Press, 1979), p. 30.

3. Thomas Merton, *The Nonviolent Alternative*, ed. Gordon C. Zahn (New York: Farrar, Straus, Giroux), p. 216

4. Henri J. M. Nouwen, *Out of Solitude* (Notre Dame: Ave Maria Press, 1974), p. 18.

5. Ibid., p. 23.

6. Max Picard, *The World of Silence*, trans. Stanley Gordon (South Bend: Regnery/Gateway, Inc., 1952), p. 18.

7. Ibid., p. 84.

8. Ellul, p. 79.

9. Henri J. M. Nouwen, *The Living Reminder* (New York: The Seabury Press, 1977), pp. 51-52.

10. John Howard Yoder, *The Politics of Jesus* (Grand Rapids: Eerdmans, 1972), p. 238.

11. Thomas Merton quoted by James Forest, "Thomas Merton's Struggle with Peacemaking," in *Thomas Merton: Prophet in the Belly of a Paradox*, ed. Gerald Twomey (New York: Paulist Press, 1978), p. 52.

12. Nouwen, *Living Reminder*, p. 54.

13. Merton by Forest in Twomey, p. 53.

14. "Waiting for a Miracle," © 1986 Golden Mountain Music Corp. Words and music by Bruce Cockburn. Taken from the album "Waiting for a Miracle." Used by permission.

15. Henri J. M. Nouwen, "Christ of the Americas," in *America*, April 21, 1984, p. 297.

16. Harvey Cox, *The Feast of Fools* (New York: Harper & Row, Publishers, 1969), p. 3.

17. Ibid., p. 3.

18. "Feast of Fools," © 1978 Golden Mountain Music Corp. Words and music by Bruce Cockburn. Taken from the album "Further Adventures Of." Used by permission.

19. "Dweller by a Dark Stream," © 1981 Golden Mountain Music Corp. Words and music by Bruce Cockburn. Taken from the album "Mummy Dust." Used by permission.

Chapter Twelve

1. Donald McNeill, Douglas A. Morrison, and Henri J. M. Nouwen, *Compassion* (Garden City: Doubleday & Company, Inc., 1982), p. 141.

2. Nouwen, *With Open Hands*, p. 92.

3. Thomas Merton, *New Seeds of Contemplation* (New York: New Directions Books, 1961), p. 123.

4. McNeill, *Compassion*, p. 4.

5. Thomas Merton, *The Nonviolent Alternative*, ed. Gordon C. Zahn (New York: Farrar, Straus, Giroux), p. 63.

6. McNeill, *Compassion*, p. 6.

7. Soren Kierkegaard, *The Works of Love*, trans. Howard and Edna Hong (New York: Harper & Row, Publishers, 1962), p. 24.

8. McNeill, *Compassion*, p. 20.

9. Ibid., p. 44.

10. Henri J. M. Nouwen, *Reaching Out* (Garden City: Doubleday & Company, 1975), p. 43.

11. Kierkegaard, *The Works of Love*, p. 316.

12. Ibid., p. 75.

13. Thomas Merton, *The Hidden Ground of Love,* ed. William H. Shannon (New York: Farrar, Straus, Giroux, 1985), p. 141.

14. Will D. Campbell, *Forty Acres and a Goat* (Atlanta: Peachtree Publishers Ltd., 1986), p. 166.

15. Ibid., p. 167.

Chapter Thirteen

1. Donald P. McNeill, Douglas A. Morrison, Henri J. M. Nouwen, *Compassion* (New York: Doubleday, 1982), p. 119.

2. Henri J. M. Nouwen, *The Way of the Heart* (New York: The Seabury Press, 1981), p. 79.

3. Douglas V. Steere, *Together in Solitude* (New York: Crossroad, 1982), p. 23.

4. Thomas Merton quoted by Jim Forest in *Thomas Merton: Prophet in the Belly of a Paradox,* ed. Gerald Twomey (New York: Paulist Press, 1978), p. 53.

5. Clarence Jordan, *The Cotton Patch Version of Hebrews and the General Epistles* (New York: Association Press, 1973), p. 35.

6. James H. Cone, *God of the Oppressed* (New York: The Seabury Press, 1975), pp. 159-160

7. Ibid., p. 160.

Chapter Fourteen

1. Michael Schwartzentruber, *From Crisis to New Creation* (Winfield, BC: Wood Lake Books, 1986), pp. 12-13.

2. Mary Jo Leddy, *Memories of War: Promises of Peace* (Lester & Orpen Dennys, 1989), p. 103.

3. Ibid., p. 103.

4. Ibid., p. 104.

5. Ibid., p. 104.

6. This story and its quotes are all taken from Philip Amerson, "Inside Story: A Parable," in *The Other Side* (September 1988), p. 14.

Bibliography

Amerson, Philip. "Inside Story: A Parable" in *The Other Side*, September 1, 1988.

Anonymous. *The Way of a Pilgrim*, Trans. R. M. French. London: SPCK, 1960.

Avila, Rafael. *Worship and Politics*. Trans. Alan Neely. Maryknoll: Orbis Books, 1981.

Birch, Bruce C., and Rasmussen, Larry L. *The Predicament of the Prosperous*. Philadelphia: The Westminster Press, 1978.

Bloom, Anthony. *Beginning to Pray*. New York: Paulist Press, 1970.

Boesak, Allan A. *Comfort and Protest: The Apocalypse from a South African Perspective*. Philadelphia: The Westminster Press, 1987.

The Book of Common Prayer. New York: The Seabury Press, 1979.

Buechner, Frederick. *Godric*. New York: Atheneum, 1980.

————. *The Hungering Dark*. New York: The Seabury Press, 1969.

————. *The Magnificent Defeat*. New York: The Seabury Pres, 1966.

————. *Wishful Thinking*. New York: Harper & Row, 1973.

Burkhart, John E. *Worship*. Philadelphia: The Westminster Press, 1982.

Campbell, Will D. *Forty Acres and a Goat*. Atlanta: Peachtree Publishers, 1986.

Campbell, Will D. and Holloway, James Y. *Up to Our Steeples in Politics*. New York: Paulist Press, 1970.

Cassidy, Richard J. *Jesus, Politics, and Society*. Maryknoll: Orbis Books, 1978.

Cassidy, Sheila. *Audacity to Believe*. London: Collins, 1977.

Cockburn, Bruce. "Dweller by a Dark Stream" on *Mummy Dust*. Toronto: Golden Mountain Music Corp., 1981.

————. "Feast of Fools" on *Further Adventures Of*. Toronto: Golden Mountain Music Corp., 1978.

————. "Waiting for a Miracle," on *Waiting for a Miracle*. Toronto: Golden Mountain Music Corp., 1986.

Cone, James H. *God of the Oppressed*. New York: The Seabury Press, 1975.

Cox, Harvey. *The Feast of Fools*. New York: Harper & Row, 1980.

Davenport, Gene L. *Into the Darkness*. Nashville: Abingdon Press, 1989.

Ellul, Jacques. *The Politics of God and the Politics of Man*. Trans and ed. by Geoffrey W. Bromiley. Grand Rapids: Eerdmans, 1972.

————. *Prayer and Modern Man*. Trans. C. Edward Hopkin. New York: The Seabury Press, 1970.

Fittipaldi, Silvio. *How to Pray Always Without Always Praying*. Notre Dame: Fides/Claretian, 1978.

Harkness, Georgia. *The Providence of God* (Nashville: Abingdon Press, 1960).

The Heidelberg Catechism. Philadelphia: United Church Press, 1962.

Heschel, Abraham J. *The Prophets*, vols. I & II. New York: Harper & Row, Publishers, 1962.

Hinson, E. Glenn. "A Minister's Devotional Life," in *Pulpit Digest*. March/April 1989.

Hughes, Kent and Barbara. *Liberating Ministry from the Success Syndrome*. Wheaton: Tyndale, 1988.

Jordan, Clarence. *The Cotton Patch Version of Hebrews and the General Epistles*. New York: Association Press, 1973.

Jordan, Clarence and Doulos, Bill Lane. *Cotton Patch Parables of Liberation*. Scottdale: Herald Press, 1976.

Kierkegaard, Søren. *Attack Upon Christendom*. Trans. Walter Lowrie. Princeton: Princeton University Press, 1968.

————. *The Journals of Kierkegaard*. Trans. and ed. by Alexander Dru. New York: Harper Torchbooks, 1959.

————. *Training in Christianity*. Trans. Walter Lowrie. Princeton: Princeton University Press, 1967.

————. *Works of Love*, Trans. Howard and Edna Hong. New York: Harper & Row, Publishers, 1962.

Kraybill, Donald B. *The Upside-Down Kingdom*. Scottdale: Herald Press, 1978, 1990.

Brother Lawrence, *The Practice of the Presence of God*. Old Tappan, New Jersey: Fleming H. Revell Company, 1958.

Leddy, Mary Jo. *Memories of War: Promises of Peace*. Lester & Orpen Dennys, 1989.

Leech, Kenneth. *Soul Friend*. London: Sheldon Press, 1977.

————. *True Prayer*. New York: Harper & Row, Publishers, 1980.

Lind, Millard C. *Biblical Foundations of Christian Worship*. Scottdale: Herald Press, 1973.

McNeill, Donald P.; Morrison, Douglas A.; and Nouwen, Henri J. M. *Compassion*. Garden City: Doubleday & Company, 1982.

Merton, Thomas: *The Asian Journal of Thomas Merton*. Eds. Naomi Burton, Brother Patrick Hart, and James Laughlin. New York: New Directions Books, 1973.

————. *Conjectures of a Guilty Bystander*. Garden City: Image Books, 1968.

————. *Contemplation in a World of Action*. Garden City: Image Books, 1973.

————. *Contemplative Prayer*. Garden City: Image Books, 1971.

————. *Faith and Violence*. Notre Dame: University of Notre Dame Press, 1976.

————. *The Hidden Ground of Love*. Ed. William H. Shannon. New York: Farrar, Straus, Giroux, 1985.

————. *The New Man*. New York: Farrar, Strauss, & Giroux, 1979.

————. *New Seeds of Contemplation*. New York: New Directions Books, 1972.

————. *The Nonviolent Alternative*. Ed. Gordon C. Zahn. New York: Farrar, Straus, Giroux, 1980.

————. *Thoughts in Solitude*. New York: Farrar, Straus & Giroux. 1977.

Mouw, Richard. "Being with the Lamb," in *Sojourners*. March 1981.

Nouwen, Henri J. M. "Christ of the Americas" in *America*. April 21, 1984.

————. *The Living Reminder*. New York: The Seabury Press, 1977.

————. *Making All Things New*. New York: Harper & Row, Publishers, 1981.

————. *Out of Solitude*. Notre Dame: Ave Maria Press, 1974.

————. *Reaching Out*. Garden City: Doubleday & Company, Inc., 1975.

————. *The Way of the Heart*. New York: Seabury, 1981.

Peerman, Dean. "El Salvador's Beleaguered Lutheran Bishop," in *Christian Century*, January 31, 1990.

Peterson, Eugene H. *Answering God*. New York: Harper & Row, 1989.

————. *Working the Angles*. Grand Rapids: Eerdmans, 1987.

Picard, Max. *The World of Silence*. Trans. Stanley Gordon. South Bend: Regnery/Gateway, Inc., 1953.

Postema, Don. *Space for God*. Grand Rapids: Bible Way, 1983.

Quoist, Michel. *Christ Is Alive!*. Trans. J. F. Bernard. Garden City: Image Books, 1972.

————. *I've Met Jesus Christ*. Trans. J. F. Bernard. Garden City: Image Books, 1975.

————. *Prayers*. Trans. Agnes M. Forsyth and Anne Marie de Commaille. New York: Sheed and Ward, 1963.

Rousseau, Ann Marie. *Shopping Bag Ladies*. New York: The Pilgrim Press, 1981.

Schwartzentruber, Michael. *From Crisis to New Creation*. Winfield, BC: Wood Lake Books, 1986.

Sider, Ronald J. *Rich Christians in an Age of Hunger*. Downers Grove: InterVarsity Press, 1978.

Steere, Douglas V. *Together in Solitude*. New York: Crossroad, 1982.

Stringfellow, William. *An Ethic for Christians and Other Aliens in a Strange Land*. Waco, Tex: Word Books, 1973.

————. *Instead of Jesus*. New York: The Seabury Press, 1976.

Swartley, Willard M. "Biblical Sources of Stewardship," in *The Earth Is the Lord's*. Eds. Mary Evelyn Jegen and Bruno V. Manno. New York: Paulist Press, 1978.

Task Force on World Hunger. *And He Had Compassion on Them*. Grand Rapids: Christian Reformed Board of Publications, 1978.

Twomey, Gerald, Ed. *Thomas Merton Prophet in the Belly of a Paradox*. New York: Paulist Press, 1978.

Wallis, Jim. "The Second Reformation Has Begun," in *Sojourners*. January 1990.

Weil, Simone. *Waiting for God*. Trans. Emma Craufurd. New York: Harper & Row, 1951.

Yoder, John Howard. *The Politics of Jesus*. Grand Rapids: Eerdmans, 1972.

Scripture Index

The Author

Arthur Paul Boers pastors the Windsor (Ontario) Mennonite Fellowship, a church planting project. He previously pastored in the Lincoln United Methodist Church (Chicago).

A free-lance writer, he has had over one hundred articles and reviews published in more than a dozen periodicals, including *Christian Living, Christian Ministry, Christianity Today, Gospel Herald, Leadership, The Mennonite, Mennonite Reporter, Our Family, St. Anthony Messenger, Sojourners,* and *The Windsor Star.* He is a contributing editor for *The Other Side* and received a second place award from the Evangelical Press Association for an interview with Henri Nouwen.

The first child of Dutch immigrants, he was born in Ontario and joined a Mennonite congregation at age 19. He received a B.A. from the University of Western Ontario, where he majored in philosophy (1976-1979); an M.A. in peace studies from Mennonite Biblical Seminary (1981-1983); and an M.Div. from McCormick Theological Seminary (1985-1988).

In 1980, he married Lorna Jean McDougall, a nurse. They have two children, Erin Margaret (1984) and Paul Edward (1987). He enjoys reading, birding, and the blues.